Preference, Value, Choice, and Welfare

This book is about preferences, principally as they figure in economics. It also explores their uses in everyday language and action, how they are understood in psychology, and how they figure in philosophical reflection on action and morality. The book clarifies and for the most part defends the way in which economists invoke preferences to explain, predict, and assess behavior and outcomes. Daniel M. Hausman argues, however, that the predictions and explanations economists offer rely on theories of preference formation that are in need of further development, and he criticizes attempts to define welfare in terms of preferences and to define preferences in terms of choices or self-interest. The analysis clarifies the relations between rational choice theory and philosophical accounts of human action. The book also assembles the materials out of which models of preference formation and modification can be constructed, and it comments on how reason and emotion shape preferences.

Daniel M. Hausman is the Herbert A. Simon and Hilldale Professor of Philosophy at the University of Wisconsin-Madison. He was educated at Harvard and Cambridge Universities and received his PhD in 1978 from Columbia University. His research has centered on epistemological, metaphysical, and ethical issues at the boundaries between economics and philosophy. He cofounded the Cambridge University Press journal *Economics and Philosophy* with Michael McPherson and coedited it from 1984 to 1994. He is the author of *Capital, Profits, and Prices* (1981); *The Inexact and Separate Science of Economics* (1992); *Causal Asymmetries* (1998); and *Economic Analysis, Moral Philosophy, and Public Policy* (2006, with Michael McPherson), among other titles. He has published more than 130 essays in academic journals in philosophy and economics. In 2009, Professor Hausman was elected to the American Academy of Arts and Sciences.

Preference, Value, Choice, and Welfare

DANIEL M. HAUSMAN

University of Wisconsin-Madison

CAMBRIDGE
UNIVERSITY PRESS

CAMBRIDGE
UNIVERSITY PRESS

University Printing House, Cambridge CB2 8BS, United Kingdom

One Liberty Plaza, 20th Floor, New York, NY 10006, USA

477 Williamstown Road, Port Melbourne, VIC 3207, Australia

314-321, 3rd Floor, Plot 3, Splendor Forum, Jasola District Centre, New Delhi - 110025, India

79 Anson Road, #06-04/06, Singapore 079906

Cambridge University Press is part of the University of Cambridge.

It furthers the University's mission by disseminating knowledge in the pursuit of education, learning and research at the highest international levels of excellence.

www.cambridge.org
Information on this title: www.cambridge.org/9781107015432

© Daniel M. Hausman 2012

First published 2012

A catalogue record for this publication is available from the British Library

Library of Congress Cataloging in Publication data
Hausman, Daniel M., 1947–
Preference, value, choice, and welfare / Daniel M. Hausman.
p. cm.
Includes bibliographical references and index.
ISBN 978-1-107-01543-2 (hardback) – ISBN 978-1-107-69512-2 (paperback)
1. Consumers' preferences. 2. Preferences (Philosophy) 3. Value.
4. Rational choice theory. I. Title.
HF5415.32.H38 2012
658.8'343–dc23 2011030303

ISBN 978-1-107-01543-2 Hardback
ISBN 978-1-107-69512-2 Paperback

Contents

Figures

Preface

When my son, Joshua, was three years old, he reflected on what he would like to be when he grew up. He thought maybe he would be an "aphosopher," or perhaps he would drive a gravel truck, or maybe he would "ride horses and shoot animals." Out of all the adult careers he knew, he was trying to figure out which he preferred. He has since considered other alternatives, and he is not a philosopher nor a truck driver nor a killer cowboy.

This book is about preferences, principally as they are and ought to be understood in economics, but also as they figure in everyday language and action, as they are understood in psychology, and as they figure in philosophical reflection on action and morality. It clarifies and assesses one concept of preferences and its role in explaining, predicting, and evaluating behavior and states of affairs, particularly in economics. Its assessment of what economists do – that is, of the ways in which they invoke preferences to explain, predict, and evaluate actions, institutions, and outcomes – is largely positive. Its assessment of what economists say about what they do is less favorable, and it criticizes some misconceptions that distort the interpretations economists have offered of their practice. Along the way it articulates some of the relations between the version of rational choice theory that economists employ and accounts of human action discussed by philosophers. This book also assembles the materials out of which models of preference formation and modification can be constructed, and it comments on how reason and emotion shape preferences.

This is not an empirical study of what people prefer, what causes people to prefer what they do, or what consequences particular preferences may have. Rather than studying what people do and why they do it, I shall be looking over the shoulders of those, such as economists and psychologists, who undertake such studies. While looking over their shoulders, I will unavoidably be looking at what they look at, but my focus is on how they see things – particularly on the way in which concepts of preference enter and should enter into their vision. The following cartoon may make what I mean clearer (Figure P.1).

ix

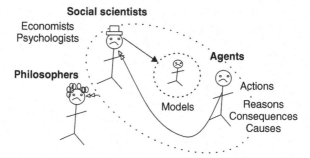

Figure P.1. Philosophers and social scientists.

In this overly simple little picture, social scientists, such as economists and psychologists, study agents, their actions, and the reasons, causes, and consequences of their actions. In studying agents, social scientists construct models. In those models, especially within economics, preferences do a great deal of work. Philosophers of the social sciences study how social scientists study agents. This book is an essay in the philosophy of the social sciences, devoted to exploring the interpretation of preferences and the role that preferences play in the understanding of action and in the appraisal of outcomes.

Preferences, like desires, play a large role in human life. People have preferences and desires about almost everything, and they incessantly express their preferences and desires in their speech and actions. Before they can talk, children reach for one toy rather than another or cry when a parent passes them into a stranger's arms. Animals also express preferences and desires, as my dog Itzhak does when he barks angrily as I prepare to leave the house.

Preferences and desires are not the same. The most important difference is that preferences, unlike desires, are *comparative*. To prefer something is always to prefer it to something else. If there are only two alternatives, one can desire both, but one cannot prefer both. Because they are comparative, preferences, unlike desires, require that one weigh alternatives. They are thus more cognitive, more like judgments, than are desires. Preferences, rather than desires, are the subject matter of this book.

A simple picture of choice and welfare, which is shown in Figure P.2, dominates mainstream economics. In this picture, the agent ranks the alternatives (represented here by different foods). Among the available alternatives, the agent chooses as far up the preference ranking as the constraints, such as prices or availability, allow. How far up the agent is able to go determines how well off the agent is. In positive economics, which explains and predicts choices and their consequences, this preference ranking governs people's choices. In normative economics, which considers which outcomes are best and what policies ought to be instituted, the objective is to move people up their preference

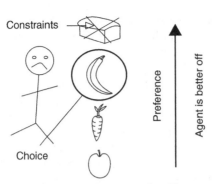

Figure P.2. Preference and welfare.

ranking. The principles of positive microeconomics are mainly generalizations concerning preferences and their implications for choice. The imperatives of normative economics specify how best to satisfy preferences. Preferences lie at the core of mainstream economic theory.

Psychologists are concerned about preferences, too, although different groups of psychologists mean different things by the term "preferences." Psychologists who collaborate with economists or who criticize mainstream economic theories of choice use the term in the same way that economists do. Other psychologists assimilate preferences to desires and theorize about choices in terms of specific motivating factors such as drives, needs, wishes, hopes, obligations, character traits, emotions, and plans. When employing a general term for what motivates people, psychologists favor "desires" over "preferences."

Preferences and desires also figure in philosophical theories of action, prudence, and morality. Philosophers have been especially concerned with the role of reasons in explaining actions and thus with the relationship between reasons on the one hand and beliefs, desires, preferences, intentions and so forth on the other hand. Philosophical accounts of prudence and well-being have often linked well-being to preference satisfaction, even though philosophers are more inclined to identify well-being with the satisfaction of rational and well-informed preferences than with the satisfaction of people's actual preferences.[1]

This book examines a concept of great importance in everyday life, economics, psychology, and philosophy. It distinguishes the notion of preference in economics from other uses of the term, and it clarifies how, on the one

---

[1] When one turns from prudence to morality (about which this book will have little to say), there is philosophical disagreement concerning the role of desire or preference. On one interpretation of Kant, morality only begins when individuals acquire the capacity to act as they judge to be right, *despite* their preferences or desires. On Humean views, in contrast, desires determine actions, and voluntary action cannot be contrary to desire.

hand, preferences depend on beliefs, desires, emotions, intentions, reasons, and values and how, on the other hand, preferences affect choices and welfare.

Why should one care about this inquiry into preferences or, in general, about what the philosopher in the cartoon in Figure P.1 has to say? Social scientists might care if they think that the philosopher will help them accomplish their tasks. Philosophers care because they want to understand how people can learn about themselves, or because they seek theories of what makes for a good life. Those who are neither philosophers nor social scientists might be interested because (like social scientists) they want to understand the causes and consequences of their choices and the reasons why they make them. A philosophical examination of social scientific inquiry can also help people understand themselves better.

This book is structured as follows. Chapter 1 is an introduction that distinguishes the concept of preference with which the book is concerned from other meanings of the term. It also sketches one way to understand how the theory of rational choice bears on the theory of actual choice, and it identifies common misconceptions concerning preferences that are criticized in later chapters. The rest of the book is divided into three parts. Part I (Chapters 2–6) focuses on the role that preferences play in the predictions and explanations of mainstream economists. After a brief introduction to the formal theory of choice in economics, Chapter 2 criticizes two misconceptions concerning preferences: that they are matters of taste and that they can be defined in terms of self-interest. Chapter 3 criticizes a third misconception: that preferences can be defined in terms of choice.

Chapter 4 is more positive. It argues that preferences in economics are and should be *total subjective rankings* – that is, subjective comparative evaluations of alternatives in terms of all relevant considerations. In showing how economists employ this conception of preferences in their explanations and predictions, Chapter 4 lays out what I call "the standard model of choice." Chapter 5 then shows how the standard model of choice is embodied in game theory. Chapters 4 and 5 show that – contrary to a fourth misconception – economists are and must be concerned with preference formation and modification. Chapter 6 concludes Part I by responding to objections to the standard model pressed by Amartya Sen.

Part II (Chapters 7 and 8) addresses the role of preferences in normative economics and in philosophical views of well-being. It argues against preference satisfaction theories of well-being. This criticism bodes ill for normative economics, which is apparently committed to the view that how well off one is depends upon how well satisfied one's preferences are. But Chapter 8 defends relying on preferences as evidence concerning what benefits people.

Part III appraises the standard model of choice and argues that economists should devote more effort to modeling preference formation and modification. Chapter 9 describes empirical shortcomings psychologists and behavioral economists have identified in the standard model of choice, and it considers their implications. The context-dependence of preferences is the central thread running through this discussion: choices depend on evaluations often made "on the fly" across multiple dimensions and with respect to a variety of criteria. Chapters 9 and 10 also discuss ways in which reasons influence preferences. Chapter 10 focuses on philosophical questions concerning how preferences ought rationally to be formed and revised. It argues that there is an unavoidable emotional element in rational preferences. Chapter 11 draws my conclusions.

This book is addressed to four audiences: economists, psychologists and other social scientists, philosophers, and interested nonacademic readers. I have kept the book short enough that material that readers do not find relevant to their particular interests will pass by quickly.[2]

I have been working on the issues addressed in this book for my whole academic career, and I cannot remember all the helpful criticisms and suggestions I have received. My apologies to those whose assistance I have failed to acknowledge. Those who have been of help over the past decade include especially Richard Bradley, Harry Brighouse, Paul Dolan, Phillip Ehrlich, Marc Fleurbaey, Catherine Hausman, David Hausman, Joshua Hausman, Robert Haveman, Daniel Kahneman, Charles Kalish, Catherine Kautsky, Cintia Retz Lucci, Philippe Mongin, Michael McPherson, Philip Pettit, Henry Richardson, Michael Rothschild, Russ Schafer-Landau, Andrew Schotter, Armin Schulz, Amartya Sen, Elliott Sober, Paul Thagard, Michael Titelbaum, David Weimer, Dan Wikler, James Woodward, and Erik Wright. My Romanell Lectures, delivered in February 2011, were drawn from this book, and I am indebted to the audiences for many helpful last-minute criticisms. Mikaël Cozic, Marc Fleurbaey, David Hausman, Joshua Hausman, Andrew Levine, Julian Reiss, Margaret Schabas, and Paul Thagard were kind enough to read the whole of the penultimate drafts of this book, and their criticisms have been invaluable. I am responsible for mistakes that remain.

Portions of the content of this book appear in previously published essays. Material from Chapters 1–4 appears in "Mistakes about Preferences in the Social Sciences," *Philosophy of the Social Sciences* 41 (2011): 3–25. Chapters 2 and 6 are derived from "Sympathy, Commitment, and Preference," *Economics and Philosophy* 21 (2005): 33–50. Chapter 3 derives from "Revealed Preference, Belief, and Game Theory," *Economics and Philosophy* 16 (2000): 99–115, and "Mindless or Mindful Economics: A Methodological Evaluation," which was published in Andrew Caplin and Andrew Schotter, eds. *Handbook of Economic Methodology* (Oxford University Press, 2008), pp. 125–51. Chapter 5

---

[2] For other useful general discussions of preferences, see Egonsson 2007, Fehige and Wessels 1998, Grüne-Yanoff and Hansson 2007, Hansson and Grüne-Yanoff 2006, and Lichtenstein and Slovic 2006a.

derives from "Consequentialism, and Preference Formation in Economics and Game Theory," *Philosophy* 59 Supplement (2006): 111–29. Chapters 7 and 8 derive from "Preference Satisfaction and Welfare Economics," *Economics and Philosophy* 25 (2009): 1–25, and *Economic Analysis, Moral Philosophy, and Public Policy* (Cambridge University Press, 2006), both of which were coauthored with Michael McPherson.

Preferences, Comparative Evaluations, and Reasons

I.I. WHAT ARE PREFERENCES?

When English-speakers talk about preferences, they do not need to use the words "prefer" or "preference." The waiter or waitress may ask Jack, "Which would you like?" rather than "Which would you prefer?" We often ask about preferences by asking people which alternative they would choose, which they like better, or which they think would be better.

There appear to be four main concepts of preference:

1. *Enjoyment comparisons.* When I say that my dog Itzhak prefers ground beef to dry dog food, or that my mother prefers yellow roses to red ones, I am talking about what gives them more enjoyment. In this sense, an agent such as Jill prefers x to y if and only if Jill enjoys x more than she enjoys y. Let us call this an *enjoyment comparison*. It may compare either overall enjoyment or enjoyment in some particular regard.

2. *Comparative evaluations.* When a politician such as Margaret Thatcher expresses a preference for one policy over another, she is not reporting her enjoyment. She is talking about which policy she judges to be superior. In this sense, an agent such as Thatcher prefers x to y if and only if she judges x to be better than y in some regard. Let us call this *a comparative evaluation*. Comparative evaluations can be *partial* – implying a ranking with respect to some specific criterion – or *total* – implying a ranking with respect to every relevant consideration. From an ideological perspective, Thatcher might object to government provision of health care, while from a political perspective, she might favor bolstering the National Health Service. When, as in this case, an agent's partial evaluations conflict, the agent must adjudicate among the different considerations if he or she is to construct a total ranking. Making a total comparative evaluation is more cognitively demanding than making an enjoyment comparison, and there is more room for mistakes.

A total comparative evaluation takes into account *every* consideration the agent judges to be relevant. Unless there is a blunder in execution, total rankings determine choices. I shall argue that preferences in economics are for the most part, and should be, total comparative evaluations.

3. *Favoring.* When people say that affirmative action calls for racial preferences, they mean that it favors racial minorities – that is, it gives them a better chance to be hired by firms or admitted by universities. There is no implication that those who implement these preferences like members of these minorities better or judge them to be superior. Favoring does not imply either an enjoyment comparison or a comparative evaluation.

4. *Choice ranking.* Finally, when a waiter asks Jill whether she would prefer the soup or the salad, he wants to know simply which Jill chooses. In this sense, Jill prefers x to y if and only if when she knows she is faced with a choice between x and y, she chooses x. Call such preferences *choice rankings*.

The four senses of "preference" often come apart: what counts as a preference given one definition does not count as a preference given another definition. For example, having recently seen the results of a cholesterol test, Jill might judge that, all things considered, the nonfat vanilla frozen yogurt is a better choice than the chocolate fudge ice cream she enjoys more. Because of laziness, habit, or mistake, Jack can choose one alternative while believing that another is better. Preference relations may be of very different kinds. Enjoyment comparisons and comparative evaluations are mental attitudes, whereas favoring and choosing are actions.

Translations of "preference" and "prefer" into other languages do not always have all of these meanings. For example, German-speaking friends tell me that the German equivalent is not used to express choices, while Chinese-speaking friends tell me that there is no good translation at all of "preference" into Chinese. These linguistic claims do not, of course, show that German-speakers are incapable of talking about what they choose. They just use different words from the ones they employ to make comparative evaluations. Nor are the Chinese incapable of comparing enjoyments, of making comparative evaluations, or of reporting what they favor or choose. But the fact that the counterparts to "prefer" and "preference" in other languages do not have all four of these meanings underlines the fact that there are four concepts here, not just one. I conjecture that English permits the use of the same word for all four concepts because they all involve favoring in some way, whether in feeling, judgment, or action.

Whether they use the word "preference" or some word in another language that roughly corresponds to it, people are constantly talking about their preferences, considering what their preferences ought to be, and inquiring about each other's preferences. Sometimes preferences require little thought.

Enjoyment comparisons require sensitivity to how one is feeling, rather than judgment. They are more like introspective reports than judgments, which may sometimes require extensive deliberation. A serious legislator's preferences among alternative social policies may depend on months of study. Even my son's early preferences reflected deliberation on his part. It may be hard to know what one prefers.

I.2. OVERALL AND TOTAL COMPARATIVE EVALUATIONS

This book focuses on preferences as *comparative evaluations*, and it takes the alternatives that people compare to be actions, their consequences, and states of affairs. I take claims about preferences among objects or properties to be elliptical statements of preferences among states of affairs. Thus, for example, to prefer Gore to Bush is to make a comparative evaluation of the states of affairs in which Gore or Bush is elected.

Individuals can evaluate alternatives in specific regards (i.e., a Bush presidency is better from the perspective of affluent taxpayers), or they can make *overall* or *total* evaluations. In everyday usage, preferences are typically "overall" comparative evaluations. In an overall evaluation, agents compare alternatives with respect to *most* of what matters to them rather than in some specific regard or with respect to everything that matters to them. In an overall comparative evaluation, in contrast to a total comparative evaluation, people regard some of the factors that affect their evaluation of alternatives as *competing with* preferences rather than as influencing preferences (Reynolds and Paris 1979, p. 356). For example, consider the following two statements concerning Jill:

1. Jill drank water rather than wine with dinner, despite preferring to drink wine, because she promised her husband she would stay sober.
2. Jill drank water with dinner because she preferred to do so. But for the promise she made her husband to stay sober, she would have preferred to drink wine rather than water with dinner.

The difference between these claims is illustrated in Figure 1.1. In Figure 1.1a, Jill's promise has no effect on her preference ranking. Instead, like a constraint, it rules out her preferred alternative and, jointly with her preferences, determines her action. In contrast, in Figure 1.1b, Jill's promise reverses her preferences between water and wine and affects her action exclusively via changing her preferences. The two sentences (1) and (2) might describe the same state of affairs, and everyday usage permits both of them, although (1) sounds to my ear somewhat more natural than (2). Standard usage favors taking feelings and tastes as influencing preferences, while regarding cognitively sophisticated evaluative factors, including especially moral considerations, as competing with preferences. But there are no hard and fast rules. One bad reason to favor formulation (1) is if one mistakenly thinks of moral

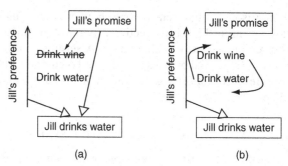

Figure 1.1. Promising and preferring.

obligation as something external to the self – like a ball and chain preventing people from doing what they truly want to do rather than as part of what determines who people are and what they value. A somewhat better reason to adopt (1) is that in their deliberations, people often treat moral considerations as constraints rather than as factors to be balanced against others. In any case, ordinary usage permits moral requirements both to compete with preference as in (1) and to influence preferences as in (2).

In everyday speech, it is natural to speak of preferences as subjective attitudes that determine how one ranks alternatives, rather than as identical to the ranking, but nothing important is at stake if I simplify and identify preferences with the rankings they determine.

To sum up: This book is concerned with preferences as comparative evaluations. Comparative evaluations can be partial, overall, or total. When people express their preferences, they are typically expressing an *overall* comparative evaluation – that is, a comparative evaluation in terms of almost all of the considerations that they find relevant. In contrast, preferences in economics are *total* comparative evaluations. As I have already noted, people sometimes use the terms "prefer" and "preference" in other ways.

I.3. PREFERENCES, REASONS, AND FOLK PSYCHOLOGY

People think about what to do and explain why others do things in terms of *reasons*. To explain why Jill went to the library, Jack might say, "Because she wanted to borrow a copy of *War and Peace*." In deciding whether to go to the library, Jack might think, "Jill is there. It's great to spend time with her." Jack explains Jill's trip to the library in terms of Jill's desire to borrow a copy of *War and Peace* and, implicitly, her belief that the library has a copy. In considering what he has reason to do, Jack cites what he believes to be a fact and what he takes to be valuable. In explaining Jill's actions, Jack employs "folk psychology," the implicit theory that people use to explain, predict, and rationalize human actions in terms of beliefs and desires. The explanations and predictions that economists give are refinements of folk psychology. Most psychologists characterize the decision making of human beings from an early age as conforming to folk psychology, and most philosophers also endorse the explanatory and predictive merits of belief-desire psychology. But there are controversies in each field. Some philosophers have gone so far as to question whether beliefs and desires exist.[1] Among those philosophers who grant that beliefs and desires help explain actions, most would argue that taking actions to be merely the causal consequence of beliefs, desires, and constraints falsifies the character of rational deliberation. From the first-person perspective of someone thinking about what to do, *reasons* are paramount. The question agents ask themselves is not "Given my beliefs and desires, what do I predict that I will do?" but "What *should* I do" or "What do I have most *reason* to do?" These may sound like moral questions, but let us set moral considerations aside. Questions about what one should do remain. To decide what to do, I try to be guided by what the facts are and by what is valuable, even though I know that my beliefs may be faulty and my desires may be nutty. That I happen to believe *P* and desire *X* is not decisive, because I can step back and question my beliefs and my desires. My awareness of a desire to do *X* does not automatically incline me to do *X* intentionally unless I can see some *reason* to do *X* (Quinn 1995; Scanlon 1998; Schapiro 2009). If I see no reason to do *X*, I will try to suppress my desire to do it. A fervent desire to eat mouse droppings sends people to a therapist rather than to their mouse-infested basement cupboards. Regardless of how value is to be understood, deliberation forces deliberators to regard values, like facts, as realities with which actions must come to terms, not as psychological crotchets.[2] From Jack's perspective, the reason to go to the library is the *fact* that Jill is there and the *value* to him of being with her, not his psychological state. Although agents can step back and ask the explanatory question "Now, why in the world did I do that?" the fundamental question from a first-person perspective is the justificatory question "What do I have most reason to do?"

Social scientists are not usually asking the first-person question. They look at behavior from a third-person perspective, where explanatory and predictive questions are paramount. But if reasons govern deliberation, third-person accounts cannot ignore reasons. Moreover, there must be a close connection between the reasons that justify actions and the beliefs and desires in terms of which others predict and explain them. The need for a connection does not imply that beliefs and desires *be* reasons. Beliefs and desires can explain why facts and values constitute reasons for action without the beliefs and desires themselves being part of the reason (Schroeder 2007, chapter 2).

---

[1] "[O]ur commonsense conception of psychological phenomena constitutes a radically false theory, a theory so fundamentally defective that both the principles and the ontology of that theory will eventually be displaced, rather than smoothly reduced, by completed neuroscience" Churchland (1981), p. 67. See also Stich (1983).

[2] As discussed in Chapter 6, the agent may also have relatively settled plans or intentions that may guide his or her deliberation. See especially Bratman (1987, 1999, 2007a).

Beliefs are linked to reasons, because beliefs purport to provide agents with facts, and facts can be reasons. The connection between desire and value is less clear. It seems that there are almost always reasons (albeit not necessarily good ones) to act on even malicious and foolish desires, such as desires to pull a fire alarm or to have "one more for the road." (But it is hard to see what reason there could be to eat mouse droppings.) Why should it be that there is typically reason to do what one desires to do? One plausible answer is that desire presents its object as in some regard valuable or "to-be-done" (Stampe 1987; Scanlon 1998; Schapiro 2009). On this view, desire motivates action and is *prima facie* evidence that there is reason to seek its object.

On this view of desire, there is an additional important distinction between desires and preferences. Desires provide *prima facie* evidence that there is reason to seek their objects. (Satisfying a whim may be reason enough if doing so is not otherwise ill-advised.) When those reasons appear not to exist, individuals take steps to purge themselves of their distorted desires. Preferences are not like this. As total or overall evaluations, they are already informed by reflection on what there is reason to do. They are the outcome of a comparative assessment, rather than inputs into deliberation like desires.

From a first-person perspective, facts and values rather than beliefs and desires count as reasons. If Jill is not at the library, then Jack has no reason to go there. If he believes she is there, he thinks he has a reason, but he is mistaken. From a third-person perspective, in contrast, the "facts" (as seen by the agent) are simply the agent's beliefs and the "values" (as seen by the agent) are simply the agent's desires. So from a third-person perspective, the agent's reasons are his or her beliefs and desires. In addition, questions about the causes of behavior are, from this perspective, at least as important as questions about what justifies behavior. So the social scientist is interested in beliefs and desires (or beliefs and preferences) as both causes of behavior and reasons for behavior.

Figure 1.2 illustrates the contrasts between first-person and third-person accounts of Jack's presence at the library. The left-hand side represents the situation as Jack sees it when he is deciding to go to the library. Facts and values are reasons for action. They serve as premises in deliberation. The right-hand side represents the situation as a third party sees it. Beliefs and preferences are both reasons for action and causes of actions (as well as causes of other beliefs and preferences). As a commentary on social science (and especially economics), this book will mainly adopt a third-person perspective, and, when speaking of reasons, I shall usually take them to consist of preferences and beliefs.

Reasons for actions do not always explain actions. Jill's being at the library and the attractions of being with Jill are reasons for Jack to go to the library, whether or not they actually influence his behavior. It might be that what explains his going to the library is instead that Jack's furnace is malfunctioning, and the library is nice and warm. When Jill's presence does not influence

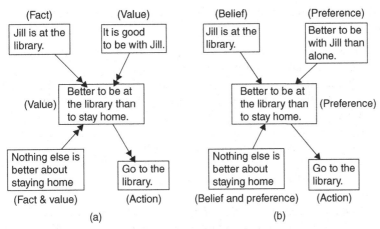

Figure 1.2. Reasons and causes.

Jack's action, it does not explain it. Donald Davidson (1963) has argued compellingly that the difference between reasons that explain actions and reasons that do not explain actions is causal: Reasons that explain actions are also causes of the actions they explain. Reasons that do not explain actions may still serve to *justify* or *rationalize* actions, to show what makes actions rational. Jack's belief that Jill was at the library gave Jack an apparent reason to go to the library, whether or not it was responsible for his going.

Given that preferences (or the facts and values that ground them) serve as reasons for actions, theories of choice should show how they do so. *Theories of choice that purport to identify reasons for choice must be theories of rational choice.* As empirical theories, they must also describe choice behavior and its causes. Although the normative adequacy of a theory of action is a separate question from its empirical adequacy, normative considerations influence empirical theorizing.

1.4. MISCONCEPTIONS CONCERNING PREFERENCES

This book argues that preferences in economics are rankings that express *total* subjective comparative evaluations and that economists are right to employ this concept of preference. Modeling behavior in terms of preferences and beliefs is an attractive path for the other social sciences as well. My quarrels are less with how economists employ the concept of preferences than with how economists have described what they are doing. This is not to say that the practice of economists has been perfect. On the contrary, mistakes in characterizing economic practice have sometimes bled into the practice itself, and I shall accordingly criticize some of what economists do and suggest ways to improve both positive and normative economics.

I shall in particular be concerned with five problematic claims concerning preferences:

1. *Arbitrariness.* Preferences are matters of taste, concerning which rational criticism or discussion is impossible.
2. *Self-interest.* People's preference rankings coincide with and are determined by their rankings of alternatives in terms of their expected self-interested benefit.
3. *Revealed preference.* Preferences in economics can be defined in terms of choices, as in revealed-preference theory.
4. *Division of theoretical labor.* Economists have nothing to say about how preferences are formed and modified and need not concern themselves with these matters.
5. *Welfare as preference satisfaction.* Welfare is the satisfaction of preferences. What makes x better than y for some agent A is A's preferring x to y.

These theses exaggerate sensible approximations or modeling strategies and distort important and defensible insights. Some, such as (2) and (3), are formulated explicitly and vigorously defended by some economists. Many economists regard claims such as (1), (4), and (5) as obvious.[3] None of the five claims is defensible. At best, some (such as (2) and (4)) are reasonable approximations in some specific contexts. In many instances, correcting these misconceptions will merely help economists understand better the sensible things they are already doing. In other cases, correcting these misconceptions should improve economics.

I.5. CONCLUSIONS

Preferences lie at the core of mainstream economics because of their connection to welfare and to choice. On the assumption that people are rational, self-interested, and knowledgeable, their preferences will both explain their

---

[3] But notice that (1) and (2) are inconsistent. What is best for me is subject to rational discussion. Later I shall discuss explicit formulations of (2), (3), and (5). As an example of (1) (the arbitrariness view), Mas-Colell et al. (1995) write in their authoritative graduate text, "The first [approach] treats the decision maker's tastes, as summarized in her *preference relation*, as the primitive characteristic of the individual" (p. 5, italics in the original). Lionel Robbins expresses the division-of-labor thesis (4): "Why the human animal attaches particular values in this sense to particular things, is a question which we do not discuss. That is quite properly a question for psychologists or perhaps even physiologists" (Robbins 1984, p. 86). More recently, Becker and Stigler phrase the division-of-labor view rather contemptuously: "On the traditional view, an explanation of economic phenomena that reaches a difference in tastes between people or times is the terminus of the argument: the problem is abandoned at this point to whoever studies and explains tastes (psychologists? anthropologists? phrenologists? sociobiologists?)" (Becker and Stigler 1977, p. 76).

choices and reflect what will benefit them. Understanding preferences better helps one understand the achievements and the challenges of economics. A better understanding of preferences should be of use to other social scientists, too, many of whom face a choice between modeling human action as governed by preferences and beliefs or as driven by diverse motivating factors. This book should also clarify some of the relations between abstract work in action theory and empirical theorizing about human action. This inquiry concerning preferences aims to illuminate one path through the tangled terrain of human action, emotion, desire, belief, and well-being.

PART I

PREFERENCES IN POSITIVE ECONOMICS

Since preferences are central to mainstream economics, one would expect economists to be explicit about what preferences are. One would expect textbooks to define "preferences" or to distinguish carefully between different notions of preferences. But in fact, economists say little about what preferences are. One finds instead axioms governing preferences and their relations to choices, with little in the way of interpretation. The five chapters that make up Part I provide this interpretation. They explore the formal theory of choice to which mainstream economists are committed, what that theory implies about what preferences are, and how economists use that theory to predict and explain choices. Chapter 2 presents the axioms of ordinal utility theory and their implications concerning preferences, and it criticizes the identification of preference with self-interest. Chapter 3 criticizes revealed-preference theory, insofar as it attempts to define preferences in terms of choice. Having cleared away erroneous interpretations, Chapter 4 defends a construal of preferences that is consistent with how economists employ the concept to explain and predict choices. Chapter 5 explores the use of this notion in game theory. Chapter 6 addresses Amartya Sen's challenge to this interpretation. The five chapters in Part I focus exclusively on the role of preferences in predicting and explaining behavior. The equally important role preferences play in the theory of welfare will be discussed in Part II.

11

2

Preference Axioms and Their Implications

Economics relies on standard axioms concerning preference and choice. Section 2.1 of this chapter presents the most important of these. Section 2.2 explores their implications for the interpretation of preferences. The conditions on preferences presented in Section 2.1 are the axioms of "ordinal utility theory," and, as Section 2.1 explains, they guarantee that people's preferences can be represented by utility functions. Section 2.3 discusses the relationship between theories of people's actual preferences and choices and theories of rational preferences and choices. Section 2.4 argues that preferences cannot be defined in terms of expected self-interested benefits.

2.1. THE AXIOMS OF ORDINAL UTILITY THEORY

The axioms of ordinal utility theory are the core of positive economic theory, and they also constitute a fragmentary theory of rationality. Economists sometimes place other constraints on preferences, about which I shall have something to say in Chapter 4, but the axioms of ordinal utility theory are central. The following axioms are standard[1]:

(*Completeness*) For all x, y in X, either $x \succeq y$ or $y \succeq x$ or both.
(*Transitivity*) For all x, y, and z in X if $x \succeq y$ and $y \succeq z$, then $x \succeq z$.

"X" is the set of alternatives over which agents have preferences – commodity bundles in the case of consumer choice theory – and x, y, and z are alternatives

---

[1] These are quoted from Mas-Colell et al. (1995), p. 6. This is one of the two main graduate microeconomic textbooks. The other, by Hal Varian, states these axioms in exactly the same way but like most presentations of ordinal utility theory includes two additional axioms:

(*Reflexivity*) For all x in $X, x \succeq x$.
(*Continuity*) For all y in X $\{x: x \succeq y\}$ and $\{x: x \preceq y\}$ are closed sets (Varian 1984, pp. 111–12).
Reflexivity is trivial and arguably a consequence of completeness, whereas continuity, which is automatically satisfied for any finite set of alternatives, is needed to prove that preferences can be represented by a continuous utility function. The reflexivity and continuity axioms are not relevant to the issues this book tackles.

13

in X. According to Mas-Colell et al. (1995, p. 6), "We read $x \geq y$ as 'x is at least as good as y'" (see also Varian 1984, p. 111). This definition of "$x \geq y$" is surprising, because the axioms are supposed to govern *preferences*, not judgments of goodness. It is better to read "$x \geq y$" as "the agent either prefers x to y or is indifferent between x and y." "$x > y$" means "the agent prefers x to y," and "$x \sim y$" means that the agent is indifferent.

In contrast to Varian, who presents the axioms as claims about people's actual preferences, Mas-Colell et al. (1995) maintain that completeness and transitivity are axioms of rationality: People's preferences are *rational* if they are complete and transitive. But because they are presenting a theory of people's actual preferences, they must also maintain that, to some extent, people's preferences are in this sense rational, and that the axioms are (to some degree of approximation) true of actual preferences.

The ordinal representation theorem proves that when people's preferences satisfy completeness, transitivity, and further technical conditions,[2] they can be represented by a continuous utility function that is unique up to a positive order-preserving transformation (Debreu 1959, pp. 56f). The "utility" of an alternative merely indicates the alternative's place in an agent's preference ranking. It is not something people seek or accumulate.

Here is a simple way to understand how a utility function "represents" preferences and what it means for it to be unique up to a positive order-preserving transformation. Suppose that an agent, Jill, who has preferences over a finite set of alternatives, adopts the convention of listing the alternatives on lined paper with preferred alternatives in higher rows and alternatives among which she is indifferent in the same row. Because Jill's preferences are complete, every alternative must find a place on the list. Because Jill's preferences are transitive, no alternative can have more than one place. Given such a list, one can assign numbers arbitrarily to rows, with higher rows getting higher numbers. Any numbering of the rows that is consistent with the ordering is an ordinal utility function. The numbers – the utilities – merely indicate where alternatives are located in Jill's preference ranking. Utility is not pleasure or usefulness or anything substantive at all. It is merely an indicator.

Figure 2.1 provides an illustration. The ordered list of alternatives is represented here by drawings of foods. U and U' are two of the infinite number of utility functions that assign higher numbers to alternatives in higher rows, and the same number to alternatives in the same row. The numbers are arbitrary apart from their order.

The theory of choice economists employ relies on two additional axioms, even though these are seldom stated explicitly as axioms. For example,

---

[2] In one version of the theorem, proven by Debreu (1959, pp. 56f), the additional technical conditions consist of reflexivity, continuity, and that the set of bundles of the k commodities be a connected subset of R^k (the k-dimensional space of real numbers). A subset of R^k is "connected" if it is not the union of two nonempty disjoint and closed subsets of R^k.

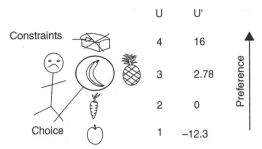

Figure 2.1. Ordinal utility.

economists maintain – and Mas-Colell et al. (1995, p. 12) purport to prove – that if preferences are rational, then choices should be consistent.[3] To defend this claim requires some axiom linking preference to choice. Here is one way to state this axiom:

(Choice determination) Among the alternatives they believe to be available, agents will choose one that is at the top of their preference ranking.[4]

So, in Figure 2.1, Jill chooses the banana rather than an apple because she prefers it to the apple. She does not choose the bread, despite preferring the bread to the banana, because no bread is available or because bread is too expensive. Because she is indifferent between the banana and the pineapple, she could just as well have chosen the pineapple.

To reach the conclusion that rational preferences imply consistent choices across different contexts requires an additional axiom concerning preferences (McClennen 1990). An anecdote attributed to Sidney Morgenbesser illustrates one aspect of the problem. According to Wikipedia:

After finishing dinner, Sidney Morgenbesser decides to order dessert. The waitress tells him he has two choices: apple pie and blueberry pie. Sidney orders the apple pie. After a few minutes the waitress returns and says that they also have cherry pie at which point Morgenbesser says "In that case I'll have the blueberry pie." (http://en.wikipedia.org/wiki/Sidney_Morgenbesser)

Morgenbesser's supposed preferences are obviously not incomplete, and they are also not intransitive, because transitivity concerns preferences over a single set of alternatives. Transitivity says nothing about how preferences over

---

[3] Consistency is defined by the weak axiom of revealed preference discussed in Section 3.1 of the following chapter. The basic idea is that if an agent chooses x when y is available, then the agent should never choose y from a set of alternatives that includes x.

[4] Mas-Colell and colleagues never state such an axiom explicitly. Varian (1984, p. 115) expresses it informally as "Our basic hypothesis is that a rational consumer will always choose a most preferred bundle from the set of feasible alternatives." The reference to belief, which is often left implicit, is necessary, because an agent can prefer x to y, yet choose y when x is available if the agent does not know that x is available.

one set of alternatives {apple pie, blueberry pie} should be related to preferences over a different set of alternatives {apple pie, blueberry pie, cherry pie}. If rational preferences are to imply consistent choices, then they must satisfy some additional condition. "The idea is that the choice of x when facing the alternatives {x, y} reveals a proclivity for choosing x over y that we should expect to see reflected in the individual's behavior when faced with the alternatives {x, y, z}" (Mas-Colell et al. 1995, p. 10).

Other features of the context than the availability of alternatives may also influence preferences. For example, many people prefer hot chocolate to beer in the winter and beer to hot chocolate in the summer. Such preferences, unlike Morgenbesser's, seem reasonable, but they apparently rule out the existence of a stable ranking of alternatives. In addition, as Chapter 9 explains, psychologists and behavioral economists have found that people's preference rankings depend heavily on a further element of context: the reference point from which alternatives appear to be losses or gains. If individuals are to have a stable preference ranking of alternatives that can be used to predict their choices as the set of alternatives, the environment, and the reference point change, all these forms of context independence must be ruled out. So one needs a further axiom requiring "stability" or context independence:

(Context independence) Whether an agent prefers x to y remains stable across contexts.

This axiom (like completeness and transitivity) is not meant to exclude the possibility that agents can change their minds and alter their preferences. It is meant to exclude Morgenbesser's pie preferences, the weather dependence of preferences between beer and hot chocolate, and dependence on a reference point. Context independence is a troublesome axiom, because some kinds of context dependence are common, and some kinds appear to be reasonable. One way to reconcile the existence of apparently context-dependent preferences such as those between beer and hot chocolate with the context independence axiom is to take the description of alternatives to include "everything that matters to the agent" (Arrow 1970, p. 45). Whether hot chocolate > beer depends on the weather, but hot chocolate and beer are not the only features of the alternatives that matter. Preferences among more complex alternatives such as {hot weather, beer} and {cold weather, hot chocolate} do not depend on the weather. It is a stretch, however, to suppose that people have preferences among such fully specified alternatives. Furthermore, taking the objects of preferences to be complete descriptions of all relevant aspects of the alternatives could eviscerate the context independence axiom. If Morgenbesser thought that whether cherry pie was available mattered to the choice between apple and blueberry pie, then his preferences would not violate context independence. To claim that whether cherry pie is available should be irrelevant to the choice between apple and blueberry seems to be a substantive requirement – "a rational requirement of indifference" (Broome 1991b, p. 103f) – rather than a formal requirement of consistency, and I am sympathetic to Broome's view that "Outcomes should be distinguished as different if and only if they differ in a way that makes it rational to have a preference between them" (1991b, p. 103). Luckily, when one is considering preferences over a single set of alternatives, there is no need for context independence.

I shall thus be concerned with four axioms: (1) completeness, (2) transitivity, (3) context independence, and (4) choice determination. The first two concern preferences over a single set of alternatives, whereas the third matters only when comparing preferences over different sets of alternatives or different descriptions of the same set. The fourth axiom, choice determination, relates preferences and choices. There seem to be counterexamples to all the axioms, several of which will be discussed in Chapter 9: people cannot always compare alternatives, people's rankings are rarely perfectly transitive, context often influences rankings, and people may choose an alternative that is "good enough" even if better choices are available. Yet, these axioms might appear to be reasonable approximations in specific applications.

2.2. IMPLICATIONS OF THE AXIOMS FOR THE UNDERSTANDING OF PREFERENCES

Choice determination has two important implications concerning the interpretation of preferences. First, it implies that preferences are not just judgments. They motivate action. If Jill knows that x is feasible, and she prefers x to all other feasible alternatives, then Jill chooses x.[5] Second, because preferences *determine* choices, they must take into account *everything* relevant to choice. If, as in everyday usage, Jill's preferences leave out factors that influence her choices, such as moral commitments, then her preferences will not determine her choices. Choice determination implies that preference rankings are not partial rankings. Preferences express total comparative evaluations, and they are intrinsically motivating.

The axioms have three other important implications. First, they imply that preferences, unlike wants or wishes, are always comparative. To say that Jill wants x and wants y leaves it open whether she prefers x to y or y to x, or whether she is indifferent. Conversely, the fact that Jill prefers x to y leaves it open whether Jill wants x. Jill might dread x, but still regard it as less bad than y.

Second, the axioms place enormous cognitive demands on agents. Although it would be possible to satisfy the axioms merely by virtue of

---

[5] If x and y were commodity bundles, this claim might appear to be false. Jill might have chosen a banana because it is cheaper than bread, even though she prefers bread. This is not a counterexample, because economists take price as determining the availability or feasibility of a consumption choice rather than as a factor affecting preferences. Although this is not the way economists think of consumer preferences, one could also regard price as one of the properties of the alternatives that determines preferences among them.

having a remarkably finely tuned gut, the only plausible way to have a complete, transitive, and context-independent ranking of alternatives (or some reasonable approximation thereto) is to adjudicate among competing considerations. Thus, although Mas-Colell et al. (1995) maintain that preference relations summarize the decision-maker's tastes (p. 5), they also maintain that "[i]t takes work and serious reflection to find out one's own preferences. The completeness axiom says that this task has [already] taken place" (p. 6). A complete and transitive preference ranking of the complex alternatives people face would be a remarkable intellectual achievement. It must be the outcome of an unmodeled process of exhaustive comparative evaluation. The axioms render the first of the misconceptions concerning preferences – that they are arbitrary matters of taste, not subject to rational consideration – highly implausible.

Third (as mentioned previously), the "alternatives" among which people have preferences cannot be ordinary options such as eating one or two scoops of ice cream. Whether Jack prefers to eat two scoops of ice cream rather than one depends on whether he has just eaten a large dinner or is currently on a diet. Thus, Jack cannot be said to have a stable preference for one scoop or two. To have preferences that satisfy the axioms, the alternatives over which preferences are defined must specify everything that matters to the agent – which will, of course, be a great deal more than whether there are one or two scoops of ice cream.

To take preferences to be defined over bundles of commodities, economists suppose that consumers are comparing two states of the world x and y alike in everything that matters other than the fact that in x the agent consumes commodity bundle x^*, whereas in y the agent consumes bundle y^*. If nothing is relevant to preferences between x and y other than the composition of x^* and y^*, then economists can treat preferences as if they were defined over the commodity bundles. Notice that this means that prices have no influence over preferences among commodity bundles. Consumer choice theory instead takes prices and incomes as jointly fixing the constraints on choices. To assume that preferences can be defined over commodity bundles rests on the assumption that the value to individuals of commodity bundles does not depend on anything apart from the composition of the bundle. But as the example of preferring beer in the summer and hot chocolate in the winter illustrates, this assumption is false. To suppose that preferences depend exclusively on the commodity bundles requires that one either ignore such dependencies or suppose that nothing relevant to preferences other than the commodity bundles varies.

The alternatives or options that I take to be ranked by preferences specify everything *relevant* to preference. As already mentioned, specifying what is relevant may require substantive commitments concerning when indifference is rationally required. This view of the objects of preference places additional cognitive demands on individuals, because whether agents prefer x to y depends not just on "local" properties of x and y, such as whether x is giving $300 to Oxfam and y is purchasing a $300 television. This preference may depend in addition on how much money others are contributing to Oxfam, what work other charities are performing, what television programs are being broadcast, what other televisions or electronic devices the agent already owns, and so forth. To have complete and transitive preferences over such complex alternatives requires more knowledge than anyone is likely to have. When there are uncertainties (as there always are), specifying the alternatives among which people have preferences presents further complications to which I return in Chapter 4 when I discuss the role of beliefs in the formation of preferences.

The axioms of ordinal utility theory say nothing about *what* people prefer. People who long for pain and suffering could satisfy the axioms as easily as those who pursue their own interests. Positive economic theory supplements the axioms of ordinal utility theory with axioms concerning the content of preferences such as the claim that people prefer more commodities to fewer. I shall not discuss these additional axioms, which say little about the concept of preference itself.

The axioms governing preference imply that preferences are rankings of complete states of the world in terms of everything relevant to choice. They are cognitively demanding and action-guiding.

2.3. RATIONALITY AND PREFERENCES

As explained in Chapter 1, any account of choice that attempts to explain and predict people's choices by their reasons must show how the factors it takes to be reasons justify choices. Accordingly, the axioms governing preferences can also be read (as Mas-Colell and colleagues read them) as imposing conditions on rational choice. What connection is there between rationality and the four axioms?

1. Completeness is a boundary condition on rational choice. An inability to compare alternatives is not itself a failure of rationality, but when people are unable to compare alternatives, they are unable to make a choice on the basis of reasons.
2. If preferences are (as I shall argue) total evaluations, then they imply judgments about what is better or more choice-worthy; and as John Broome (1991a) has argued, transitivity is then implied by the logic of comparative adjectives such as "better than" or "more choice-worthy than." If preferences place alternatives along some ruler measuring "betterness" or "choiceworthiness," then intransitive preferences are logically inconsistent and hence irrational.[6]

[6] If, on the other hand, preferences are partial pairwise comparisons instead of total evaluations, then there is no reason to expect them to be transitive. See Temkin (1987) and Tversky (1969).

3. If the alternatives that Jack ranks specify everything "relevant" to preference, then whether z is available has no relevance to the merits and drawbacks of x and y. If Jack violates context independence and his preference between x and y depends on whether z is available, then his preferences depend (irrationally) on factors that ought to be irrelevant.

4. That choices be determined by preferences is *not* demanded by rationality. Indeed attempting to adhere to choice determination may sometimes be irrational. As Herbert Simon argues (1982), it is rational to adopt strategies that reduce the cognitive burden of decision making and take account of the limits to one's information and information-processing abilities. Adopting these strategies sometimes leads people to choose options that are inferior to feasible alternatives. In addition, it may be rational to carry through with one's intentions or plans, even if changing course would be more advantageous. All one can say in defense of the rationality of choice determination is that agents should not choose x when they know they could have chosen y and are confident that, all things considered, y is the better choice to make.

These comments explain why economists regard ordinal utility theory as both a fragment of a positive theory that explains and predicts choices and as a fragment of a theory of rational choice that specifies conditions that preferences must satisfy in order to justify choices. This theory of rational choice purports to be purely *formal* and to say nothing about what things it is rational to prefer.

Although not part of utility theory, many economists think that it is rational to prefer what will make oneself better off. Self-interest is implicit in the view that individuals prefer larger commodity bundles to smaller. To claim that it is rational to be self-interested would be part of a substantive as opposed to a merely formal theory of rationality.

2.4. PREFERENCES AND SELF-INTEREST

Let us begin our consideration of how economists understand preferences by considering the influential views of Amartya Sen, a Nobel Laureate in economics, who is also a major contemporary philosophical voice. Sen defends no single definition of "preference." Instead, he emphasizes that economists have used the word to refer to different things. Among these different concepts of preference, Sen believes that two are most important. He writes:

Certainly, there is no remarkable difficulty in simply defining preference as the underlying relation in terms of which individual choices can be explained.... In this mathematical operation preference will simply be the binary representation of individual choice. The difficulty arises in interpreting preference thus defined as preference in the usual sense with the property that if a person prefers x to y then he must regard himself to be better off with x than with y. (Sen 1973, p. 67)

A "binary *representation* of individual choice" specifies which alternative is chosen from each pair. Like a list of what someone chooses, a binary representation of choices cannot *explain* choices. This notion of preference as a choice ranking, which coincides with what economists call "revealed preference," is the subject of Chapter 3. Second, there is what Sen labels "the usual sense" of preference, whereby a person prefers *x* to *y* if and only if the person believes that he or she is better off with *x* than with *y*. In the same vein, Daniel Kahneman and Richard Thaler (2006) maintain that economists typically equate what people choose with what they predict they will most enjoy. One might read Sen as merely offering the empirical generalization that what people prefer matches what they believe to be best for themselves, rather than as suggesting a definition of preference. But other comments show that Sen regards expected advantage as one *meaning* of preference. For example, he writes, "Preference can be defined so as to preserve its correspondence with choice, or defined so as to keep it in line with welfare as seen by the person in question" (Sen 1973, p. 73; see also Sen 1980, p. 442). Let us call this sense of preference "expected advantage ranking." Expected advantage rankings express partial comparative evaluations of alternatives in terms of expected advantage.

Sen repeatedly warns against conflating choice rankings and expected advantage rankings:

[T]he normal use of the word permits the identification of preference with the concept of being better off, and at the same time it is not quite unnatural to define "preferred" as "chosen." I have no strong views on the "correct" use of the word "preference," and I would be satisfied as long as both uses are not *simultaneously* made, attempting an empirical assertion by virtue of two definitions. (Sen 1977, p. 329)

Sen avoids legislating the meanings of words (see, for example, Sen 1991a, p. 588; 1991b). Rather than defending a single interpretation of the word "preference," he maintains that economists should recognize that the term has many meanings. Sen counsels awareness of ambiguity rather than proposing a cure, because he fears that regimentation would encourage among economists an overly simple view of evaluation and choice.

In Chapter 6, I argue against Sen that economists should employ a single concept of preferences as total comparative evaluations. Whether or not I am right about that, Sen is mistaken to suggest that "the normal use of the word permits the identification of preference with the concept of being better off." Expected advantage cannot be what people *mean* by preference, because there is no contradiction in maintaining that people's preferences depend on many things that people do not expect to bear on their own well-being. People do not apportion their donations to disaster relief by calculating how much those donations will contribute to their own well-being. Nor do they decide whether to give a truthful answer to a stranger asking directions by considering what answer is most in their interest. When, in the grip of road rage, Jack rams the car that has cut him off, he is thinking about harming somebody else, not benefitting himself. Consider the humdrum instrumental decisions that fill daily life. People often have no idea how the alternatives bear on their interests, and in making these decisions, people are not calculating their advantage. For example, when grading student papers, I have thousands of decisions to make concerning what comments to write in the margins. Regardless of whether my determination to do a conscientious job is motivated by an expectation of personal benefit, specific choices such as whether to write "ungrammatical" rather than "awkward" in the margin next to a particular sentence are not directed by expectations about what will benefit me.

The mere *possibility* that people have preferences among alternatives without considering how they bear on their interests, or that people sometimes sacrifice their interests to accomplish something that matters more to them, shows that preferences cannot be defined in terms of well-being. And these are not mere possibilities: People often prefer x to y without believing that x is better for them than y is.

Many economic models take people to be self-interested, and for specific purposes such models are often useful. But self-interest must not be built into the meaning of preferences. By taking preferences to be total comparative evaluations (as they must if preferences are to determine choices), economists allow preferences to be influenced by everything agents regard as relevant to their choices, whether these be moral or aesthetic considerations, ideals, whims, fantasies, or passions of all sorts. Only people who are never motivated by passions, fantasies, whims, ideals, or moral and aesthetic concerns, and who are moreover able to pretend that they can always judge how alternatives bear on their own interests, could rank alternatives entirely in terms of their expected self-interested advantages.

Given that what people prefer does not always match what they judge to be best for themselves, expected advantage could not possibly be a tenable meaning of "preference." Sen's remarks thus leave us with only one alternative: choice ranking, or the theory of revealed preference, which deserves a chapter to itself.

3

Revealed-Preference Theory

As we saw in Chapter 2, Amartya Sen offers two main interpretations of preference rankings: as rankings of alternatives in terms of expected self-interested benefits and as rankings that represent choices. Chapter 2 argued that preferences cannot sensibly be defined in terms of expected benefit. That leaves the subject of this chapter, the view that preferences constitute the ranking of alternatives that is implicit in people's choices. As Gul and Pesendorfer (2008, p. 7) put it, "In the standard approach, the terms "utility maximization" and "choice" are synonymous." Under the label of "revealed-preference theory" many economists have espoused this view of preferences.

In criticizing revealed-preference theory, I shall argue that Gul and Pesendorfer mischaracterize the practice of economics, not that they correctly characterize a mistaken practice. Economists do not and cannot employ a notion of preference defined in terms of choices. The problem lies not in what economists do, but with what some economists, including distinguished economists such as Gul and Pesendorfer, think they are doing. The conception of preferences that economists in fact employ takes them to be subjective states that determine choices only in conjunction with beliefs. Economists cannot substitute a notion of preference defined in terms of choices for this subjective conception. This chapter aims to clear away the confusions caused by defenders of revealed-preference theory and to help economists conceive of their practice more clearly.

Much of what I argue may appear beside the point to economists, who often take "revealed preference" to mean nothing more than inferring preferences from choices and beliefs or from market data. ("The indirect market methods discussed in this chapter are based on *observed behavior*, that is, *revealed preference*" [Boardman et al. 2010, p. 341].) Hal Varian takes revealed-preference theory to address the following questions:

Given a set of observations of prices and chosen bundles, (p^t, x^t) for t = 1, ... , T, we can ask four basic questions:

Consistency. When is the observed behavior consistent with utility maximization?

Form. When is the observed behavior consistent with maximizing a utility function of particular form?

Recoverability. How can we recover the set of utility functions that are consistent with a set of choices?

Forecasting. How can we forecast what demand will be at some new budget? (Varian 2006b, pp. 102–03)

I am not criticizing these inquiries. My argument is instead that these inquiries are entirely compatible with a view of preferences as total subjective comparative evaluations that are linked to choices only via beliefs. The object of my criticism is the conceptual claim that preferences can be *defined* by choices.

In carrying out these empirical inquiries and in speaking of "revealed preference," most economists have not been concerned with such conceptual niceties. Economists who maintain that preferences are revealed by choices are more concerned with making inferences about preferences from data concerning choices than with how preference should be defined. Consequently, they have meant rather different things by "revealed preference," and they have often failed to distinguish among these meanings. Those who first defended revealed-preference theory, such as Paul Samuelson (1938) and Ian Little (1950), maintained that economists can define preferences in terms of actual choices. Their motivation was in part philosophical: Because preferences are "in the head" and cannot be directly observed, Samuelson and Little felt that reliance on them was unscientific. (For a contrasting view of Samuelson's objectives, see Mongin [2000].) These empiricist scruples are in accord with positivist views in philosophy of science that were influential at that time. Because choices are observable, showing that claims about preferences are entailed by claims about choices allays empiricist qualms about theories concerning preferences. Call this version of revealed-preference theory "actual revealed-preference theory."

A second version of revealed-preference theory, which I shall call "hypothetical revealed-preference theory," has been defended by economists such as Ken Binmore (1994), albeit often without distinguishing it clearly from Samuelson's and Little's version. In Binmore's view, whether an agent prefers x to y can be defined by whether an agent would ever choose y from any set of alternatives including x. Whether the agent actually faces a choice between x and y is irrelevant. Preferences should instead be defined in terms of statements about what agents *would* choose.

Finally, there is the uncontroversial view that choices are evidence of preferences – that *given information about people's beliefs*, one can infer their preferences from their choices. For example, *if* one attributes to Jill the belief that she can purchase U.S. government bonds, then one can infer from her purchases of corporate bonds that she does not prefer government bonds to corporate bonds. However, if she does not know that government bonds are for sale, one can draw no conclusions concerning her preferences among corporate and government bonds. Let us call this view of the belief-dependent link between preference and choice "belief-dependent revealed-preference theory." Unlike actual and hypothetical revealed-preference theory, belief-dependent revealed-preference theory *denies* that preferences can be defined in terms of choices. The only sense in which it takes preferences to be "revealed" by choices is that preferences can be inferred from choices and beliefs. Empirical work recovering utility functions from choice behavior in fact relies on premises concerning beliefs and does not define preferences by choices.

3.1. ACTUAL REVEALED PREFERENCES AND THE REVELATION THEOREM

Actual revealed-preference theory is an interpretation of formal results explored initially by Paul Samuelson (1938, 1947), generalized and developed by many others (especially Houtthakker [1950]), and elegantly summarized by Arrow (1959), Richter (1966), and Sen (1971). Actual revealed-preference theory identifies preferences with actions. Many economists have mistakenly concluded that the literature on revealed preferences succeeds in *proving* the central claim of actual revealed-preference theory, that x >$_A$ y (A prefers *x* to *y*) if and only if A never chooses *y* from any set, including $\{x, y\}$, that includes *x*. Thus, for example, Henderson and Quandt (1980, p. 45) take it as proven that "the existence and nature of her [an agent's] utility function can be deduced from her observed choices among commodity bundles," and Gravelle and Rees (1981, p. 115) believe it has been shown that "the utility maximizing theory of the consumer and the revealed-preference theory are equivalent."

Here is a statement of the fundamental technical result: First, some definitions:

- *X* is a nonempty finite set of alternatives.
- *S* is a nonempty subset of *X*.
- *K* is the set of all nonempty subsets of *X*.
- $C(\text{ß})$ is a set-valued function from each *S* in *K* to a nonempty subset $C(S)$ of *S*. $C(S)$ is the "choice set," the set of alternatives that the agent chooses from *S*.
- *R* is a two-place relation such that *xRy* if and only if *x* is in the choice set of some set of alternatives that includes *y*. "*R*" is supposed to be interpreted as "weak preference," so that *xRy* if and only if x ≥ y.
- $C^R(S)$ is the set of all the members of *S* that bear the relation *R* to every member of *S*.

Given the intended interpretation of *R*, $C^R(S)$ is the set of "top alternatives" – the alternatives preferred to every member of *S* that does not belong to $C^R(S)$.

In addition to these definitions, one axiom is needed, the "weak axiom of revealed preference" (WARP):

If there exists $S \in K$ such that $x \in C(S)$ and $y \in S$ but $y \notin C(S)$, then there is no $S' \in K$ such that x and $y \in S'$ and $y \in C(S')$.

In other words, if x and y are both alternatives in the set S, but only x is in the choice set, $C(S)$ of S, then there is no other set S' containing x and y where y is in the choice set of S'.

Given the definition of R, WARP may be restated:

If there exists $S \in K$ such that $x \in C(S)$ and $y \in S$ but $y \notin C(S)$, then it is not the case that yRx.

In other words, if x and y are both alternatives in some set S, x is in the choice set of S and y is not, then it is not the case that yRx. Given the intended interpretation of R, what this means is that if x and y are both in S, but only x is in $C(S)$, then x > y.

The Revelation Theorem: WARP implies that (a) R is complete, (b) R is transitive, and (c) that $C^R(S) = C(S)$.[1]

In other words, if an agent's choice is consistent (i.e., satisfies WARP), then one can impute to the agent a "preference" relation R that is complete and transitive and that implies the agent's choice.

On the intended interpretations, $C(S)$ consists of the alternatives an agent chooses from S and xRy means that $x \geq y$ – that x is preferred to y or that the agent is indifferent between x and y. Given these interpretations, the revelation theorem establishes that preferences can be defined in terms of choices when choice behavior satisfies WARP. But are economists entitled to these interpretations of $C(S)$ and xRy? The theorem does not prove anything about how its functions and relations should be interpreted, and it does not establish that R coincides with or could replace the notion of preferences that economists employ.

---

[1] The proof can be sketched simply:

    (a) Because for all x,y, $C(\{x,y\})$ is not empty, R is complete. If x is in $C(\{x,y\})$ and y is not, then xRy and not yRx. If y is in $C(\{x,y\})$ and x is not, then yRx and not xRx. If both x and y are in $C(\{x,y\})$, then it is both the case that xRy and yRx.

    (b) Suppose that xRy and yRz. Given the definition of R and WARP, xRy implies that there is no set of alternatives whose choice set includes y but not x, and yRz implies that there is no set of alternatives whose choice set includes z but not y. So xRy and yRz jointly imply that $C(\{x,y,z\})$ (which is by definition nonempty) consists either of $\{x\}$, $\{x,y\}$, or $\{x,y,z\}$, and all three of these possibilities imply xRz. So R must be transitive.

    (c) If $x \in C(S)$, then by the definition of R, for all $y \in S$, xRy, and so $x \in C^R(S)$. Conversely, if for any S, $x \notin C(S)$, then because the choice set is nonempty, some other alternative $y \in C(S)$. That means that yRx and it is not the case that xRy, and so $x \notin C^R(S)$. So $C^R(S) = C(S)$.

Some economists take the revelation theorem to show that economists can dispense with the notion of preference altogether. On this view, the theorem shows that anything economists need to say about the behavior of individuals can be said in the language of choice (Mas-Colell et al. 1995, p. 5). In this way, economists with strict empiricist scruples, such as Samuelson or Little, defended the scientific credentials of economics. Other economists regard the correspondence between choice and preference as legitimating talk of subjective states. In Sen's (1973, p. 244) words, "The rationale of the revealed-preference approach lies in the assumption of revelation and not in doing away with the notion of underlying preferences." Neither of these interpretations of the theorem is defensible. Talk of preferences cannot be eliminated without gutting economics, and the logical relations between $C(S)$ and xRy does not reveal "underlying preferences."

3.2. CRITIQUE OF ACTUAL REVEALED-PREFERENCE THEORY

Actual revealed-preference theory faces multiple objections,[2] but I shall discuss only the two most important. First, if preference is defined by choice, then where there is no choice, there is no preference. Actual revealed-preference theory thus limits preferences to those alternatives among which agents in fact choose (Reynolds and Paris 1979, p. 356). This limitation means that economists cannot make use of premises concerning the preferences of agents for things they cannot choose, such as lower inflation or a higher salary from their boss, to explain or predict economic behavior. Restricting preferences to what I call "final preferences" – preferences among the immediate objects of choice – would cripple economics. There would be nothing to be said about how expectations or preferences among the consequences of choices affect choices. The only thing economists could say would be that people chose among the feasible actions whatever they most preferred. Moreover, because preference is defined by choice, to say that people choose among the feasible actions whatever they most prefer would mean nothing more than that people choose consistently.

The second problem with actual revealed-preference theory is that preferences influence choices only via beliefs. Preferences cannot be defined by choice, because the same choice reflects different preferences when beliefs differ. For example, at the end of *Romeo and Juliet*, Romeo enters the tomb of the Capulets and finds Juliet apparently dead. She is in fact alive, but he does not know that she took a potion that merely simulates death. Unwilling to go

---

[2] For important criticisms see Sen (1971; 1973). For example, if people choose only a few times from {x, y}, how can one distinguish preference from indifference? How can one distinguish indifference from violations of WARP? Why should one believe, as actual revealed-preference theory implies, that individuals prefer what they choose to every alternative they could have chosen?

on living with Juliet dead, Romeo takes poison and dies. The alternatives he actually faces are death or eloping with Juliet – although, tragically, he does not know that. From the set of alternatives actually available to him – {death, eloping with Juliet} – Romeo chooses death. If choice defines preference, then Romeo prefers death to eloping with Juliet. But, of course, he does not prefer death to life with Juliet. His choice does not reveal his preference, because he is mistaken about what the alternatives are among which he is choosing. It is perfectly possible to prefer x to y yet to choose y from the set $\{x, y\}$, because, like Romeo, one mistakenly believes that one is choosing between y and something other than x.

One might object that the set of alternatives among which Romeo is choosing should be defined by his beliefs. We should regard him as choosing between death and life without Juliet rather than between death and eloping with Juliet, and his choice then correctly reveals his preference for death over living without Juliet. But allowing beliefs to determine the set of alternatives among which agents choose does nothing to mitigate the conclusion that preferences cannot be defined simply by choice regardless of belief.

Economists have paid little attention to this crucial problem – that revealed-preference theory falsely implies that beliefs are irrelevant to the relation between choice and preference – because they so often restrict their models to circumstances where what people believe coincides with what is truly the case. If beliefs match the reality, then to predict choices, economists need only know people's final preferences and the actual circumstances. But the fact that economists need not mention beliefs when they assume that all beliefs are true does not imply that beliefs do not matter. Preferences cannot be defined by choices, because preferences cannot be limited to the immediate objects of choice and because they can be inferred from choices only given premises concerning beliefs.

3.3. WHY NOT REDEFINE PREFERENCES IN TERMS OF CHOICE?

Since the revelation theory demonstrates that the choice set coincides with the set of feasible alternatives that maximizes R, why not just define $x \geq y$ as xRy? Given this definition, a revealed-preference theorist should maintain that Romeo in fact prefers death to a life with Juliet. However unsatisfactory this may be as literary criticism and however much it offends ordinary usage, Romeo in fact chose death when he might have had life with Juliet. Unless he violates WARP – and given the nature of his choice, his future consistency is guaranteed – his choice reveals his "preference." Revealed-preference theorists are not trying to capture the everyday meaning of the term. They are employing a technical concept that is defined in terms of choice. If speaking this way confuses outsiders, economists can stop talking about preferences and talk exclusively in terms of choices.

Economists are entitled to define their own technical concepts and to proscribe the use of everyday concepts, but they should then use the concepts they define rather than the concepts they proscribe. In fact, economists cannot make do without a concept of subjective preferences, which cannot be defined by choices. For example, given the underlying preferences of investors for high returns and low risks, both the booming market for securitized mortgages and its collapse when new information about risks became available were predictable. The "underlying" preferences for high returns and low risks are not revealed preferences; they are subjective evaluations that, when combined with beliefs, result in choices. Revealed-preference theorists could not have predicted what the consequences would be of information concerning the real risks of mortgage-backed securities.

Given that economists are more concerned with the consequences of choices than with the prediction or explanation of choices, a revealed-preference theorist might shrug off this limitation as unimportant. But this limitation is crushing. Consider, for example, another scene from literature, this time from *Pride and Prejudice*. Midway through the novel, Darcy is overcome by his love for Elizabeth and proposes marriage to her, despite the undesirable features of the connection, such as Elizabeth's vulgar mother and her silly younger sisters. Elizabeth thinks that Darcy is arrogant and unfeeling, and she bitterly turns him down. Their interaction can be modeled as the game shown in Figure 3.1.

The numbers there are (ordinal) utilities – that is, indicators of preference. Higher numbers indicate more preferred alternatives. The first number in each pair expresses Darcy's utility, and the second number expresses Elizabeth's utility. Darcy moves first and can either propose or not propose. Not proposing ends the game with the second-best outcome for both players.[3] If Darcy proposes, then Elizabeth gets to choose whether to accept or reject his proposal. Rejecting the proposal is the best outcome for Elizabeth and the worst for Darcy, whereas accepting it is best for Darcy and worst for Elizabeth. Darcy would not have proposed if he knew Elizabeth's preferences.

Some of the preferences in Figure 3.1 are revealed by choices. Elizabeth's refusal reveals that she prefers rejecting to accepting the proposal. But other preferences, which are needed to define the game, rank alternatives between which agents do not choose. Elizabeth does not and cannot choose between (1) Darcy not proposing and (2) his proposing followed by her rejection, yet to define the game, she must have a preference between these alternatives. Darcy cannot choose whether Elizabeth accepts his proposal, yet he prefers that she does. If Darcy does not propose, Elizabeth does not get to reveal

---

[3] It is arguable whether Elizabeth preferred to receive and reject Darcy's proposal over not receiving the proposal. Whether I am right about Elizabeth's preference does not matter to the point the example makes.

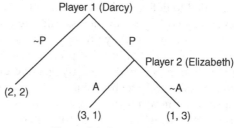

Figure 3.1. Darcy proposes.

any preferences. Yet without those preferences, there is no game. The preferences in Figure 3.1 are not revealed preferences (Rubinstein and Salant 2008, p. 119). If economists limited themselves to preferences defined by choices, they could not do game theory.

Beliefs mediate the relationship between choices and the preferences with which economists are concerned. Economists can infer preferences from choices or choices from preferences only given premises concerning the agent's beliefs. Different preferences can lead to the same action, depending on what the agent believes. Neither beliefs nor preferences can be identified from choice data without assumptions about the other. Choices can be evidence of preferences, but they do not define them.

A brief example of how this matters in practice may be useful. In a recent article, Kremer, Miguel, Leino, and Zwane attempt to determine the values placed on clean water and on averting the death of children by the population in a rural area of Kenya. They write:

A discrete choice model, in which households trade off water quality against walking distance to the source, generates revealed preference estimates of household valuations of better water quality. Based on household reports on the trade-offs they face between money and walking time to collect water, estimated mean annual valuation for spring protection is US$2.96 per household. Under some stronger assumptions this translates to an upper bound of $0.89 on households' mean willingness to pay to avert one child diarrhea episode, and $769 on the mean value of averting one statistical child death ... (Kremer et al. 2011, pp. 147–48)

Willingness to pay is a measure of strength of preference. Kremer and colleagues' claim is that by examining choices between walking further to collect water from protected springs and taking water from closer sources, they can infer that Kenyans on average are indifferent between allowing a child to die and spending no more than $769. They take their work to provide a revealed-preference estimate of the value of childhood health. However, as the authors recognize, their conclusions concerning values and preferences do not follow from the choice behavior without assumptions about beliefs. They point out, "The link between spring protection and child death – a relatively rare occurrence with multiple possible causes – may be quite difficult for households to discern in practice" (Kremer et al. 2011, p. 148). If Kenyans do not know that polluted water causes childhood diarrhea and death, no conclusions can be drawn concerning how strongly they prefer to avoid them.

3.4. HYPOTHETICAL REVEALED PREFERENCES

Instead of defining preferences in terms of an agent's actual choices, hypothetical revealed-preference theory defines an agent's preferences in terms of what the agent *would choose* if the agent were able to choose. In switching from actual to hypothetical choice, one abandons the empiricist ideal of avoiding references to anything that is not observable. How John McCain would choose to set the minimum wage in the hypothetical circumstances in which he gets to choose the minimum wage cannot be read off any choices he actually makes. It is unclear what the advantage might be of asking this odd question about hypothetical choice rather than asking what he prefers.

Hypothetical revealed-preference theory avoids restricting preferences to the actual immediate objects of choice. But it is still too restrictive. Consider the proposal game depicted in Figure 3.1 again. For this to be a well-defined game of perfect information, both players must be able to rank the three terminal nodes. But what hypothetical choices could reveal that Darcy prefers that his proposal be accepted? In the case of a marriage proposal, it matters crucially that the other person does the deciding! Preferences range more widely than hypothetical choices.

In addition, questions about what agents would choose are unanswerable without premises concerning what they believe. *Hypothetical choice is not choice.* It is instead a prediction about what someone would choose in a particular epistemic situation. Without specifying what the agent believes, one has not specified the situation in which the agent is to choose, and no prediction can be made. Predictions about what Romeo would do depend on premises concerning what he believes.

A simple game illustrates vividly that any sensible notion of hypothetical choice relies on premises concerning beliefs. Consider the normal form representation of a game shown in Figure 3.2.

The players play simultaneously – neither knows how the other has played before he or she has to make his or her own move – and the game is common knowledge. The numbers are ordinal utilities indicating preferences, with the first number indicating Jack's preferences and the second Jill's preferences. Larger numbers represent more preferred outcomes. Game theorists would note that *left* is a dominant strategy for Jill, the column player: No matter whether Jack plays *up* or *down*, Jill prefers the outcome from playing *left*. So she will play *left*. Because Jack knows what strategies are available to Jill and her preferences over the outcomes, he knows she will play *left*. Because he prefers the outcome of {*down, left*} to the outcome of {*up, left*}, he will play *down*. The outcome will be {*down, left*}, which is the unique pure-strategy

Jill

		Left	Right
	Up	1, 4	4, 3
Jack			
	Down	2, 2	3, 1

Figure 3.2. Games and hypothetical choice.

Nash equilibrium. If Jill could convince Jack that she was going to play *right*, then he would play *up*, and both players could do better (although of course Jill would do still better by double-crossing him and playing *left*). However, there is no way for Jill to get Jack to believe that she will play *right*.

Suppose that economists identified preferences with hypothetical choices, as the hypothetical revealed-preference theorist maintains, instead of taking preferences to influence choices only via beliefs. Then, if the normal form of Figure 3.2 were common knowledge, Jill would know that if she were to play *right*, Jack would play *up*. According to hypothetical revealed-preference theory, that is what Jack's preference for {*up, right*} over {*down, right*} means. Knowing this, Jill should play *right*. This reasoning is absurd: It maintains that Jack's choice magically depends on what Jill does, regardless of what Jack believes. Whether Jack plays *up* or *down* depends on his *beliefs* about what Jill does, not on what Jill in fact does. Jack's preference for {*up, right*} over {*down, right*} implies only that Jack would play *up* if he *believed* that Jill played *right*. Beliefs must be part of the analysis.[4] I doubt that hypothetical revealed-preference theorists would disagree. When purportedly defining preference in terms of what an individual would choose, my guess is they take for granted that the individual knows what alternatives are available. This makes their view sensible, but it concedes that preferences are related to choices only via beliefs and that preferences cannot be defined in terms of choices.

Economists generate predictions of choices and give explanations of choices by deriving choices from preferences *and* beliefs. Subjective preferences combine with beliefs to cause actions. Revealed preferences do not. Neither actual nor hypothetical revealed preferences do the jobs that preferences do in economics. Empirical work devoted to drawing inferences concerning

---

[4] Even if some agent such as George were correctly to believe that he faced a choice between *x* and *y*, his actual preference between *x* and *y* (which are not currently objects of choice) might differ from what he would choose, because the hypothetical change of circumstances that makes *x* and *y* available for choice might change his preferences. For example, suppose George works on an assembly line, and one of his two supervisors, Mary and Jane, is up for promotion. George hopes that Jane gets the promotion, because she has been a pain to work for, but he, of course, does not get to choose. Faced with the hypothetical, "Which would you promote if you had the choice?" George might answer, "Mary," because if he had the choice, he would regard the promotion from the perspective of someone who would be working with the candidate who was promoted rather than the candidate who was passed over.

preferences from choice behavior (which is often called "revealed-preference theory") does not presuppose or support the view that preferences can be defined by choices.

3.5. BELIEF-DEPENDENT REVEALED PREFERENCES

What the sensible work done under the banner of revealed-preference theory presupposes is merely that inferences concerning preferences can be drawn from choices given premises concerning belief. For example, Green and Osbard (1991) and Border (1992) take revealed-preference theory to maintain that preferences can be inferred from choices given premises concerning belief. The only problem is that this kind of "revealed-preference" work misleadingly suggests a commitment to defining preferences by choices when there is none. Economists should not conflate belief-dependent revealed-preference theory with either hypothetical or actual revealed-preference theory. Once beliefs are fixed, preferences (understood as total comparative evaluations) can be inferred from choices, and choices can be inferred from preferences. These inferences depend on assumptions about the constraints and the ways in which the agent individuates the alternatives (Jeffrey 1983, p. 219). The view that preferences and beliefs jointly cause actions is sensible and embedded in everyday explanatory and predictive practices. Belief-dependent revealed-preference theory is compatible with the traditional view of preferences as subjective states whose connection to choice is causal rather than definitional.

3.6. CONCLUSIONS

One cannot define preferences by choices. The connection between preferences and choices is conditional on beliefs. There is no one-to-one correspondence between preferences and choices and no possibility of defining preferences by choices. Preferences are subjective states that, jointly with beliefs, cause and justify behavior.

4

Preferences, Decision Theory, and Consequentialism

The last two chapters argued that economists should reject Sen's two definitions of preferences. Preferences cannot be defined by expected advantage or by choice. What then are preferences? What satisfies the axioms of ordinal utility and combines with beliefs to determine choices?

4.1. TOTAL SUBJECTIVE COMPARATIVE EVALUATIONS

Given the axioms of ordinal utility theory, preferences entail a complete and transitive ranking that determines choices when combined with beliefs and constraints. Because this ranking determines choices, it must be a total ranking, incorporating every factor agents take to influence their choices. As economists understand preferences, nothing competes with preferences in determining choices. Once beliefs and constraints are given, preferences are determinative.

As we saw in Chapter 3, preferences stand in no simple relationship to behavior, and even final preferences cannot be defined by choices. Preferences must instead be subjective motivational ("conative") comparative attitudes. Like the voltage in a circuit that determines the current only in conjunction with the resistance, so preferences determine choices only in conjunction with beliefs.

The interpretation of preference that fits the bill takes them to be total subjective comparative evaluations. To say that Jill prefers x to y is to say that when Jill has thought about everything she takes to bear on how much she values x and y, Jill ranks x above y. A total ranking, like any ranking, may be complete, and insofar as it is a ranking, it will be transitive. Because Jill's total subjective ranking does not leave out anything that she regards as relevant to the evaluation of alternatives, it combines with beliefs to determine her choices. It may thus be context independent and must be choice determining.

A total ranking contrasts with a partial ranking, not with an ill-considered ranking. Examples of partial rankings would be Jill's ranking of alternatives in terms of her own enjoyment or the expected benefits they will provide to her uncle. These rankings will not coincide with her total ranking unless all that mattered to Jill were her own enjoyment or the expected benefit to her uncle. Her total subjective ranking might be carefully thought out, or parts might rest on mere whim; and her ranking might collapse upon more careful reflection. Jill might be ignorant of important considerations or careless in canvassing relevant factors. Her total comparative evaluation need not be stable or rationally defensible, although it may be.

Total subjective comparative evaluation is for the most part *the* notion of preference economists and decision theorists employ.[1] It is "the underlying relation in terms of which individual choices can be explained" (Sen 1973, p. 67). In insisting on this conception of preferences, I am not criticizing the practice of economics. My objective is instead to help economists understand what they are already doing. They should regiment their language and reserve the word "preference" for this single usage. In contrast to Sen, I, like John Broome (1991a), favor *prescribing* how the word "preference" should be used in economics. Given that my prescription matches most of current practice, it is easy to follow.

This notion of "preference" does not conform to the ordinary usage of the word, which permits some factors that influence choices, including especially moral commitments, to compete with preferences rather than to influence choices via influencing preferences. In the usage of economists, in contrast, everything that influences choices, apart from beliefs and constraints, does so via influencing preferences. By replacing the everyday concept of an overall comparative evaluation with the concept of a total comparative evaluation, economists have defined a more precise notion with a tighter connection to choice.

In some circumstances, it is a reasonable approximation to maintain that people's total subjective rankings of alternatives match their rankings of alternatives in terms of expected advantage. In that case, economists can make inferences about expected advantage from preferences and inferences about preferences from expected advantage. But economists should not follow Sen and take expected advantage to be "the usual sense," or indeed any *sense* at all, of preference. Similarly, when Jack's total ranking is limited to the objects among which he is choosing and Jack knows what alternatives are available, then his total subjective ranking will match the ranking that is implicit in his choices. Because this coincidence between Jack's choice and his final preferences depends on his knowing what alternatives he faces, preferences cannot be defined by choices.

---

[1] Philosophers and decision theorists have employed this notion as well: "But throughout, I am concerned with preference *all things considered*, so that one can prefer buying a Datsun to buying a Porsche even though one prefers the Porsche qua fast (e.g., since one prefers the Datsun qua cheap, and takes that desideratum to outweigh speed under the circumstances). *Pref* = preference *tout court* = preference on the balance" (Jeffrey 1983, p. 225).

4.2. USING PREFERENCES TO PREDICT AND EXPLAIN CHOICES: THE STANDARD MODEL

Economists conceive of preferences as total subjective rankings rather than as choice rankings because they need to relate choices to beliefs and to evaluations of things that are not objects of choice. For example, people buy different cars when they learn that the price of gasoline is likely to stay high. If all that consumer choice theorists could say about why an agent purchased one thing rather than another was that the consumer preferred to make that purchase, there would be no Nobel Prize in economics. If all that game theorists could say about why individuals play one strategy rather than another is that they prefer that strategy, game-theory texts would be very brief.

How do preferences over consequences and properties of alternatives combine with beliefs to determine final preferences? How do final preferences combine with beliefs to determine choices? Unlike primitive urges, people's preferences depend on their beliefs concerning the character and consequences of the objects of their preferences. Adapting some useful terminology that Sen (1970, chapter 5) introduced in a discussion of values, one can distinguish "basic" preferences, which are independent of beliefs, from nonbasic preferences that depend on beliefs. Almost all preferences are nonbasic. Even a matter of taste, such as a preference for one flavor of ice cream over another, is sensitive to beliefs about the health effects of the different flavors or about the environmental consequences of their production.

In what I call, tendentiously, "the standard model" of choice in economics, shown in Figure 4.1, choices depend directly on three things: preferences among the objects of choice, beliefs about which of these are available for choice, and facts about what can be chosen. The arrows represent causal relations. Constraints obviously influence actions: No matter how much one would like to fly and how firmly one believes that one can, flapping one's arms vigorously will never get one off the ground. Constraints also affect actions via an agent's recognition of them (and hence the arrow from constraints to beliefs). Most people do not try to fly because they know they cannot. In addition to causing choices, beliefs and preferences influence other preferences as, for example, when my aversion to headaches coupled with my beliefs about the properties and consequences of taking aspirin lead me to prefer to take some. Although not discussed by economists, final preferences (preferences among the alternatives among which one is choosing) may also influence preferences among the consequences of those alternatives. For example, strongly preferring the foie gras in a French restaurant to his mother's chopped chicken liver, Jack may temper his preference for humane treatment of fowl rather than simply overruling it. Hence the dotted arrow from preferences among actions to preferences among their characteristics and consequences.

I maintain that Figure 4.1 depicts the view of choice mainstream economists hold.

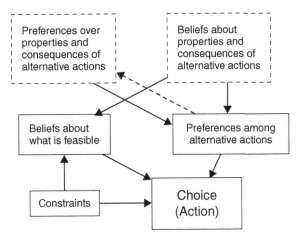

Figure 4.1. The standard model of choice.

Some economists disagree on the grounds that positive economics takes preferences as *given* and leaves questions about what shapes preferences for psychologists, other social scientists, or perhaps even biologists. This view constitutes the fourth of the five misconceptions about preferences listed in Chapter 1. If economists truly had nothing to say about what shapes final preferences – if they left the top two boxes in Figure 4.1 out of their stories – their predictions and explanations of choices would be trivial. Economists had better have something to say about how beliefs and preferences over properties, outcomes, or states lead to final preferences, and they do. Both game theory, which is discussed in Chapter 5, and expected-utility theory offer formal accounts of how beliefs and preferences shape final preferences, and books and articles in economics are full of informal examples.

4.3. EXPECTED-UTILITY THEORY

Expected-utility theory can be regarded as a formal version of the standard model, in which preferences among actions can be literally calculated from beliefs and an evaluation of the possible consequences of actions. Expected-utility theory adds further axioms to ordinal utility theory and reinterprets the objects of choice as lotteries or as functions from uncertain states of affairs to outcomes. The most important of the additional axioms is the independence axiom, which says, roughly, that an agent's preferences between two lotteries that differ in only one prize should match the agent's preferences between the two prizes. Let "$[(x, p), (y, 1 - p)]$" denote the lottery that results in x (which may itself be a lottery), with probability p and y with probability $1 - p$. The independence axiom says that for all lotteries $x, y, z, w,$ and w', where $w = [(x, p), (y, 1 - p)]$ and $w' = [(z, p), (y, 1 - p)]$, $w \succeq w'$ if and only if $x \succeq z$. Because the

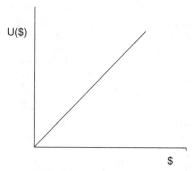

Figure 4.2. Linear preferences.

additional axioms of expected-utility theory have no important implications concerning the interpretation of preferences, I shall not discuss them here. For formal presentations of expected-utility theory, see Harsanyi (1977, chapter 3) and Savage (1972).

The most important result is the cardinal representation theorem, which says that if an agent's preferences satisfy the axioms of expected-utility theory, then they can be represented by utility indices that have two properties in addition to indicating preference ranking. First, preferences that satisfy the axioms can be represented by "expected utilities" – indices that have *the expected-utility property*: The utilities they assign to lotteries are the sum of the utilities of the payoffs weighted by their probabilities. If $w = [(x,p), (y, 1 - p)]$, then $U(w) = pU(x) + (1 - p)U(y)$. The utilities represent the preferences of some agent. The probabilities can either be objective or they can express the subjective degrees of belief of the agent.

For example, suppose that $U_j(.)$ (a utility function with the expected-utility property representing Jill's preferences) is an increasing linear function of the monetary payoff she receives. A graph with monetary payoffs on the horizontal axis and Jill's utility on the vertical axis would be a straight line sloping up to the right, as in Figure 4.2.

Suppose Jill is offered a gamble (lottery), where she will receive the same number of dollars as the number of dots showing on the top of a die she rolls. What she most prefers is that the die lands with a six on top, then a five, and so forth. If the die is not weighted, the expected monetary value of the gamble is \$3.50 (that is, $(1/6) \cdot [\$1 + \$2 + \$3 + \$4 + \$5 + \$6]$). Because Jill's expected utility is (I have assumed) an increasing linear function of money, let $U_j(\$x)$ be the simplest function – that is, simply x. In that case, the expected utility of a roll of the die would be $(1/6) \cdot 1 + (1/6) \cdot 2 + (1/6) \cdot 3 + (1/6) \cdot 4 + (1/6) \cdot 5 + (1/6) \cdot 6$ or 21/6 = 3.5 "utils." This means, among other things, that Jill is indifferent between this gamble and one that pays off \$4 if a fair coin lands heads and \$3 if the coin lands tails. Jill prefers the gamble of rolling the die to the outcome of the die coming up with one, two, or three dots on the top face, but she prefers the outcome of the die coming up with four, five, or six dots showing to the gamble. One can calculate Jill's preferences between the gamble and the payoffs.

The second crucial property of expected utilities is that if U_j is an expected-utility function that represents Jill's preferences, then U_j' is also an expected-utility function that represents Jill's preferences if and only if $U_j' = aU_j + b$, where a and b are real numbers and $a > 0$. ($aU_j + b$ with $a > 0$ is called "a positive affine transformation" of U_j.) So any positive affine transformation of $U_j(\$x) = x$, such as $U_j(\$x) = 2x + 1$, would represent Jill's preferences just as well. The utility of any lottery will still be a sum of its prizes weighted by their probabilities. With $U_j(\$x) = 2x + 1$, the utility of the lottery described above is 8, which is again exactly halfway between 7, the utility of getting \$3 for sure, and 9, the utility of getting \$4 for sure. On the other hand, a function such as x^3, which is a positive monotone transformation of an expected-utility function but not a positive affine transformation, does not preserve the ranking of lotteries.[2]

The fact that if U and U' are expected-utility functions, then $U' = aU + b$, with $a > 0$, makes comparisons of sums and differences of expected utilities independent of which expected-utility function one chooses to represent an agent's preferences. As some simple algebra confirms,[3] if $U'(x) = aU(x) + b$ with $a > 0$, then $U(x) - U(y) > U(w) - U(z)$ if and only if $U'(x) - U'(y) > U'(w) - U'(z)$. So one can compare the expected utility of alternative actions by summing the utilities of their consequences weighted by the probabilities of the consequences.[4]

The fact that expected utilities can be added or subtracted does not imply that utility is some "stuff" that people seek, such as the pleasure that Jeremy Bentham thought all choices aimed at. Although expected utilities indicate

---

[2] $U_j(\$x) = x^3$ still represents Jill's preferences for outcomes involving no risk or uncertainty, but it does not have the expected utility property and does not represent her preferences among lotteries. With this utility function, the utility of the above lottery would be 73.5 – one-sixth times $(1 + 8 + 27 + 64 + 125 + 216)$. $73.5 > 64$, which is the utility of the \$4 payoff if the die lands with four dots up. Taking $U_j(\$x) = x^3$ to be Jill's expected utility function would lead to the false conclusion that Jill prefers the lottery to \$4 for sure.

[3] If $U'(x) - U'(y) > U'(w) - U'(z)$ and $U'(x) = aU(x) + b$, then $aU(x) + b - aU(y) - b > aU(w) + b - aU(z) - b$. So $a[U(x) - U(y)] > a[U(w) - U(z)]$. If $a > 0$, then $U(x) - U(y) > U(w) - U(z)$. Similar steps demonstrate the converse.

[4] The expected utility of a lottery reflects both diminishing marginal utility and risk aversion. If marginal utility of money diminishes – that is, additional dollars contribute less to Jack's preference satisfaction when he has more money – then the utility of \$100,000 may be less than twice the utility of \$50,000, and Jack will prefer \$50,000 for certain to a lottery that has a 50–50 chance of paying off \$100,000 or nothing. Lotteries also involve risk, and because he is averse to risk, Jack may prefer \$50,000 for certain to a lottery with a 50–50 chance of paying off \$100,000 or nothing, even if the utility of \$100,000 were twice the utility of \$50,000. Having mentioned this complication, I shall say little more about it.

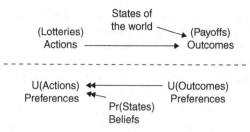

Figure 4.3. Means-end reasoning.

intensity as well as ranking, they are still only indices that represent features of an agent's preferences.

The axioms of expected-utility theory also imply that an agent's degrees of belief satisfy the axioms of the theory of probability and that an agent's preferences among lotteries will be appropriately sensitive to the agent's degrees of belief. For example, consider the lottery $L = [(x, p_k), (y, 1 - p_k)]$, where the probabilities are Jack's degrees of belief. Suppose that L^* is another lottery with the same prizes, but in L^* Jack believes that the probability of his receiving x is q_k, where $q_k > p_k$. If Jack prefers x to y, then the expected utility of L^* will be larger than the expected utility of L, and Jack will prefer L^* to L.

4.4. WHAT DOES EXPECTED-UTILITY THEORY ACCOMPLISH?

When students first study expected-utility theory, they are inclined to interpret it as a theory that derives preferences among actions from beliefs and preferences among their possible consequences – that is, as an elaboration of the standard model and of means-end reasoning. Seeing expected-utility theory this way involves two related causal claims, depicted in Figure 4.3.

In interpreting expected-utility theory as means-end reasoning, one regards the outcomes of actions as causal consequences of actions and states of the world, and one takes preferences among actions to derive from preferences among their outcomes and the probabilities of the states of the world that determine the outcomes. The arrows pointing left in Figure 4.3 have two heads, because preferences among actions are caused by, derived from, and justified by preferences among outcomes and probabilities of states of the world. For example, suppose that Jack is willing to pay $45 for a gamble that pays off $100 if a fair coin lands heads and nothing if it lands tails. Knowing $U_k(\$100)$ and $U_k(\$0)$, an economist can calculate the expected utility of the gamble ($U_k(\$100)/2 + U_k(\$0)/2$), which must be larger than $U_k(\$45)$, since Jack accepted the gamble. Whether or not Jack did any calculating, the economist's calculation of the utility of the gamble provides a causal explanation for why Jack was willing to pay $45 for the gamble.

The causal arrows in Figure 4.3 might be questioned, because *expected-utility theory says nothing about causation*. It is not explicitly an account of means-end reasoning. For example, suppose that Oedipus employed expected-utility theory when deciding to marry Jocasta. He had a strong aversion to marrying his mother, but he mistakenly attached such a low probability to that possibility that he preferred marrying Jocasta to not marrying her. Incest plays the same role in the calculation of the expected utility as the possible causal consequences of marrying Jocasta, but marrying his mother was not a causal consequence of marrying Jocasta. (It was the very same event.) Expected-utility theory merely relates preferences over the "payoffs" of lotteries and degrees of belief to preferences over lotteries. The relations between lotteries and their payoffs are typically causal, but no causal interpretation is built into expected-utility theory itself (Savage 1972, pp. 13–14).[5]

Many economists would maintain that expected utilities only *represent* preferences. In their view, expected-utility theory says nothing about what *determines* them and is not a formal implementation of what I called the standard model of choice. In support of this interpretation, economists can point out first that if preferences are, as an axiom asserts, complete, then agents must already know their preferences among lotteries. If they need expected-utility theory to figure out what their preferences are, then their preferences would not be complete. Second, although it might be possible to use expected-utility theory to guide one's preferences in tricky situations,[6] expected utilities could not be assigned to outcomes in the first place unless agents already had preferences over at least some lotteries. Third, suppose that w is the lottery $[(x,p),(y,1-p)]$, yet there is no expected utility representation of Jill's preferences such that $U_j(w) = pU_j(x) + (1-p_j)U_j(y)$. All that expected-utility theory says about such a possibility is that Jill's preferences must violate one or more of the axioms. To make her utilities conform to the axioms, Jill must change some preference or belief. But expected-utility theory gives her no reason to change the expected utility she assigns to the lottery rather than to change the expected utility of one of the prizes or to revise her subjective probabilities.

---

[5] The fact that expected-utility theory abstracts from questions about causation has led to criticism. Suppose with Fisher (1959) that smoking and lung cancer were related as effects of a common cause rather than as cause and effect. Then, although smoking would convey the bad news that one is more likely to come down with lung cancer, the probabilistic association between smoking and lung cancer would give one no reason not to smoke. If decision theorists had no indicators of the existence of the common cause with which to screen off the statistical relevance of smoking, the expected utility of not smoking for most people would be lower than the expected utility of smoking; and decision theory would mistakenly advise against smoking. See Gibbard and Harper 1978, Lewis 1981, Skyrms 1982, Eells 1982, Hitchcock 1996, and Joyce 1999.

[6] When faced with complicated problems, calculation can avoid mistakes. In a famous encounter, Maurice Allais asked Leonard Savage to state his preferences among two pairs of alternatives. The preferences Savage expressed, like the preferences many other people express when faced with this problem, violated the independence axiom. One might take Savage's response as refuting the independence axiom, or one might take it (as he did) as an argument for using calculations of expected-utility theory to guide one's preferences.

If expected-utility theory were a theory of preference formation, on the other hand, it would tell her to revise her preference for *w*.

The orthodox view, which I shall shortly criticize, is accordingly that economics is not committed to the standard model of choice because economics has nothing to say about where preferences come from or how agents should modify their preferences if they violate the axioms of expected utility. In the orthodox view, there is a division of labor, whereby economics concerns itself with agents whose preferences are complete and already conform to the axioms. Questions about how agents came to have those preferences and about how to modify preferences that violate the axioms are for others to tackle.

4.5. CONSEQUENTIALISM AND STANDARD CHOICE THEORY

Those who maintain that expected-utility theory says nothing about preference formation are right to point out that expected-utility theory *need not* imply anything about the formation of final preferences; but they are wrong to suggest that actual applications do not say anything about preference formation. For example, although simplified versions of the theory of the firm take as given the preferences of firms for larger rather than smaller net returns, they do not take as given final preferences over input mixes or level of output. On the contrary, the theory of the firm shows how the firm's preferences among mixes of inputs or levels of output *depend on* prices, technological possibilities, and the firm's preference for larger net returns. In predicting that in response to an increase in the minimum wage, firms will cut back on their employment of unskilled workers, economists are implicitly making claims about how the preferences of firms over alternative mixes of inputs into production are formed.

Some economists may object that it is illegitimate to speak of final preferences – that is, preferences over the immediate objects of choice, such as mixes of inputs or levels of output. What firms prefer are larger profits or a greater market share, not the specific actions that implement these general preferences. To be sure, firms make specific choices in order to achieve greater net returns or market share, just as players choose strategies in order to achieve an outcome of a game that they prefer to others. However, some economists might argue that speaking of preferences among these detailed alternatives misunderstands economic theory.

Like the defender of revealed-preference theory, those who press this objection deny that final preferences derive from beliefs and other preferences. But rather than limiting preferences to final preferences, as the revealed-preference theorist urges, those who press this objection deny that economists should countenance final preferences. Neither way of pretending that there is no story to be told about how beliefs and preferences among the consequences of actions influence final preferences is defensible. What grounds could there be to deny that players have preferences over strategies or that entrepreneurs have preferences among techniques of production? The most one can say is that because there is so little distance between final preference and choice, final preferences are of little interest. But the fact that final preferences are uninteresting – that they are almost as tightly connected to choice as the revealed-preference theorist pretends – is no argument that they do not exist.

Applications of the theory of the firm, such as the argument that increases in the minimum wage decrease employment of unskilled workers, are instances of an explanatory and predictive strategy, which I call "consequentialism." By "consequentialism," I do not mean the ethical view that actions and policies should be evaluated in terms of the impartial total goodness of their consequences. I mean instead the claims about preference formation implied by the standard model. More specifically, a model of choice is consequentialist if and only if:

1. An agent's final preferences derive from
   a. the agent's beliefs about the properties and consequences of the alternatives, and
   b. the agent's preferences over these properties and consequences.
2. An agent's choices causally depend on the agent's beliefs and the agent's final preferences among the alternatives that, given the constraints, can be chosen.

Given beliefs and distal preferences, economists derive final preferences. Through deliberation, attitudes spread out and transfer from consequences and characteristics to actions. The standard model of choice in economics is consequentialist.

Economic theorizing does not always require any theory of preference formation. Consumer choice theory treats prices and incomes as constraints that winnow the set of commodity bundles among which individuals can choose rather than as influences on preferences. So it can make do with predetermined preferences among commodity bundles, unmodified by market forces. But this case is atypical.

Consequentialism requires a distinction between those preferences it takes as given and those preferences it undertakes to explain and to predict. Although the theory of the firm includes a consequentialist account of how preferences among input mixes or levels of output are formed, it says nothing about what determines preferences among net returns or market shares. To preserve some remnants of a division of labor, whereby questions about how preferences are formed and changed are kept out of economics proper, consequentialist views distinguish between (final) preferences among actions such as choices of production techniques and preferences among the consequences and properties of actions. The latter are givens, and those committed to a division of labor can argue that economists have nothing to say about how they are formed or modified. But the former are not given. They derive from beliefs and preferences among the properties and consequences of actions. Consequentialism functions as a structure for explaining and predicting final preferences. Although consequentialism is not a plausible view of all of practical reasoning, it is a reasonable first approximation in some economic applications.[7]

A consequentialist view of the traditional theory of the firm is a sensible approximation. Although it embodies an account of preference formation, the consequentialist can insist that economics addresses only the formation of final preferences, not of the preferences among consequences that (jointly with beliefs) determine final preferences. An important theoretical point remains: *If economists want to say more about choice among some set of alternative actions than that people choose what they prefer, they need to say something substantial about what determines what people prefer.* In treating preferences as total comparative evaluations, economists have essentially trivialized the connection between final preference and choice. Provided that the agent knows what alternatives he or she faces, choice and preference coincide. Unless economists have something nontrivial to say about preferences, they have nothing nontrivial to say about choice. Furthermore, insofar as they are committed to consequentialism, which derives preferences among actions from preferences among their properties and consequences, economists must concede a good deal to the naive student who sees applications of expected-utility theory as deriving preferences among actions from preferences among their outcomes.

Beliefs are as important as distal preferences in determining final preferences. For example, the announcement that Vioxx significantly increases the risk of strokes and heart attacks changed many people's preferences between taking Vioxx and taking aspirin by changing their beliefs about the consequences of taking one pill or the other. Rather than the modest view that utilities and subjective probabilities only *represent* the agent's preferences, most people – including most economists – would regard people's preferences among the alternative anti-inflammatory medications as *determined by* their underlying preferences (concerning stomach upset, heart attacks, strokes, and joint pain and flexibility) and by their beliefs about the consequences of taking alternative medicines.

We are thus back to the standard model and to the naive view that applications of expected-utility theory show how preferences among uncertain prospects depend on subjective probabilities and preferences among the prospect's outcomes or aspects. One cannot consistently maintain that expected-utility theory merely represents Jill's preferences while also endorsing the consequentialist view that Jill's preferences among actions depend on her

---

[7] This sense of consequentialism is closely related to Peter Hammond's notion (1988a, 1988b), but he is mainly concerned with consequentialism as a rationality condition rather than as a structure for predictive and explanatory theories of choice.

preferences among their properties and consequences and her beliefs about
what they are likely to be.

4.6. ATTRIBUTES AND PREFERENCES

"Consequentialism," may be a misleading name because it suggests that final
preferences depend exclusively on beliefs and preferences concerning the
causal consequences of choices. But, as already illustrated by Oedipus' fateful
choice, the aspects of choices that people care about extend beyond causal
consequences. Kelvin Lancaster (1979, p. 17) writes: "Individuals are interested in goods not for their own sake but because of the characteristics they
possess, so that the demand for goods is derived and indirect and depends
on preferences with respect to characteristics and on the technical properties that determine how characteristics are embodied in different goods." (See
also Lancaster 1966.) He then sketches a theory whereby consumer choices
depend on the consumer's budget, prices of commodities, preferences over
characteristics, and relationships between commodities and characteristics
that are mediated by consumption activities. The relations between commodities and their characteristics are typically not causal. The size and location of
a house, which may explain why Jack buys it, are not effects of the house. The
absence of a specifically causal relationship is, however, no barrier to deriving
preferences among commodities from the values of their characteristics.[8] I
have defined consequentialism broadly enough that derivations of final preferences from the values of the characteristics of alternatives also count as
consequentialist.

Multi-attribute utility theory (Keeney 1982, 1992; Keeney and Raiffa 1993;
Nelson 1999) and "hedonic pricing" (Rosen 1974; Malpezzi 2002) thus count
as consequentialist, though the latter is concerned with prices rather than
preferences. Multi-attribute utility theory is most often employed as a part of
"decision analysis," a largely prescriptive theory designed to assist in decision
making (Keeney 1982). But multi-attribute utility theory has also been used
to address empirical questions in economics and marketing (Nelson 1999).
Multi-attribute utility theory conceives of actions and their consequences as
bundles of attributes. The beliefs and values of agents with respect to these
attributes determine their final preferences and actions (Chapman 2003,
p. 1210). If a possible consequence, c, of an action has n relevant characteristics

---

[8] Gary Becker defends a related view in which market goods are regarded as inputs into a
"household production function" whose outputs are the object of consumer preferences
(Stigler and Becker 1977). Preferences among market goods can be derived from preferences among the outputs of the household production function and information about that
function, and properties of the household production function can be inferred from market
behavior. Although the outputs of a household production function are not quite the same
thing as attributes, there are analogies, and Becker provides another way to model preference
formation and modification.

or attributes, $(c_1, c_2, ..., c_n)$, then $U_J(c)$ (which represents where c ranks in Jill's preferences) depends on the values of c's attributes $(u_J(c_1), u_J(c_2), ..., u_J(c_n))$ (Keeney and Raiffa 1993, pp. 14, 31f, 48). Multi-attribute utility theory assumes that values can be assigned to attributes and that preferences among consequences can be calculated from these values.

Although not intended as a normative theory or as an explicit account of individual preferences, hedonic pricing has a similar structure. The most important applications have been to the housing market. Economists can, for example, postulate that the rent R in a particular market at a particular time[9] depends on structural characteristics (S), neighborhood characteristics (N), location within the market (L), and contract conditions (C). R = f(S, N, L, C) (Malpezzi 2002). Presumably rents depend on these variables because preferences among apartments depend on these variables, too – although of course rents depend on factors influencing supply as well as demand. Views about preference formation are implicit in hedonic pricing. The implicit function relating preferences among apartments to their attributes, unlike the function relating preferences among lotteries to their possible outcomes does not – at least as a first approximation – rely on probabilities. One can instead suppose that the attributes of alternatives (unlike whether Jocasta is Oedipus' mother) are known with certainty. Furthermore, equations relating prices to the values of attributes will generally not be linear or additive, since the contribution that one attribute makes to the value of an alternative will not in general (even as an approximation) be independent of the level of the other attributes. If one assumes that the values of the variables are continuous, one common specification of the functional form is $\ln(R) = \alpha + \beta.\ln S + \delta.\ln N + \gamma.\ln L + \nu \ln C$, which implies that the "hedonic price" of an attribute diminishes with the level of the attribute and increases with the levels of all the other positive attributes.

Apart from some models of hedonic pricing, evaluative attitudes toward properties of alternatives play little role in mainstream economics. This is the substance of Philip Pettit's (2002) "abstraction thesis." Pettit criticizes economics for abstracting from the "desiderative structure" of folk psychology, whereby preferences among states of affairs (and actions and consequences) are explained and justified in terms of people's attitudes toward the properties of those states of affairs. That criticism does not apply to multi-attribute utility theory or hedonic pricing, which are devoted to capturing desiderative structure.

One reason why evaluative attitudes toward attributes play little role in mainstream economics is that it is difficult to capture desiderative structure formally and to derive testable implications. It is one thing to claim that preferences among states of affairs depend on attitudes toward their properties

---

[9] I am assuming that the time when the rent is observed is fixed and so have omitted the time variable in Malpezzi's example.

and quite another to define a multi-attribute utility function linking the utility of an alternative to the values of its attributes. Although there will be particular applications where it is reasonable to impose a simple functional form on a multi-attribute utility function, in general the relationship between an agent's preference ranking of x and y and his or her attitudes toward the properties of x and y will be complicated. In addition, there is little reason to suppose that Jack's evaluation of the properties of alternatives is fixed while his preferences among the alternatives themselves remain to be determined. Pettit disagrees. He maintains that "we always desire prospects for the properties we think they have" (Pettit 2002, pp. 198–99) and that "the rational agent's ultimate points of reference, his ultimate motivational bearings must be given by abstract properties rather than by concrete outcomes" (Pettit 2002, p. 207). I do not see why this must be so. Although Jack's ranking of the experiences of reading *Gulliver's Travels* and *Pilgrim's Progress* might be a function of his general liking of allegory and irony, it is also possible that he comes to value irony more highly by coming to appreciate *Gulliver's Travels* or that he learns the attractions of allegory from coming to value *Pilgrim's Progress*. Simple models may abstract from such complications, but doing so may diminish their accuracy.

Multi-attribute utility theory and hedonic pricing are compatible with the standard model shown in Figure 4.1, where final preferences depend on beliefs and preferences among both the consequences and the properties of alternatives (Fishburn 1977). When not asserting that expected-utility theory merely represents preferences, economists have generally taken the consequences on which choices depend to be causal consequences and have treated expected-utility theory as a formalization of means-end reasoning. Multi-attribute utility theory and hedonic pricing, in contrast, rely on constitutive relationships between attributes and states, acts, or consequences rather than causal connections. Yet the way in which multi-attribute utility theory accounts for preferences among actions resembles the way in which expected-utility theory accounts for preferences among actions, and economic tools and models can be (and have been) deployed to study how preferences depend on the values of the characteristics of the alternatives.

4.7. CONCLUSIONS

This chapter's inquiry into how economists use preferences and beliefs to explain and predict choices reveals tensions at the core of choice theory. Some of these are inconsistencies between what economists do and how they think about what they are doing. Many are inclined to say that expected-utility theory merely represents preferences, which are already determined, and that expected-utility theory has nothing to say about what determines preferences. Many economists would endorse the more general claim that economics has nothing to say about preference formation. Yet economists derive preferences over the immediate objects of choice from preferences over their consequences and properties and from subjective probabilities of those consequences. The practice of economists in this instance is superior to their preaching, for without such an account of preference formation, economics would have little content.

There are also tensions within the practice of predicting and explaining economic behavior. On the one hand, economists take preferences to be total subjective rankings that are complete and hence already formed. (If some of the agent's preferences remain to be determined, then the agent's preferences are not yet complete.) An agent's deliberation is then a straightforward matter of applying his or her predetermined ranking to the set of feasible alternatives. Although economists can explore the relations among an agent's preferences by means of expected-utility theory or multi-attribute utility theory, the orthodox view denies that that exploration explains how those preferences were formed. On the other hand, consequentialist explanation and prediction requires that economists derive the agent's preferences among the objects of choice from beliefs and information about preferences among their consequences or the values of the attributes of the objects of choice and their consequences. How can these two views of agents be put together? Either preferences are already given, in which case consideration of what they depend on has no role in the explanation or prediction of behavior, or a consideration of what determines preferences has a role in explaining and predicting choices, and agents should not be modeled as already possessing a complete ranking of all alternatives.

One might attempt to reconcile the opposed positions by distinguishing among different explanatory (or predictive) questions. When the question is "Why did the agent choose x?" (or "What choice is predicted?"), preferences should be taken as a given. To answer by reporting that the agent preferred x to all the other feasible alternatives conveys some information. When, in contrast, the question is "Why does the agent prefer x to y?" (or "What preferences are predicted?"), then the agent's final preferences should not be taken as given. However, this reconciliation does not save completeness: If economists address the second question – as they must – then this reconciliation implies that economists cannot always assume that the preferences of agents are complete. Economists must instead explore how preferences are formed and modified.

5

Game Theory and Consequentialism

Game theory, like expected-utility theory, predicts and explains behavior in terms of preferences and beliefs and the constraints that determine which choices are feasible. What distinguishes it from expected-utility theory is its focus on strategic interactions – circumstances in which outcomes depend on the choices of others as well as on one's own choices. In explaining and predicting choices among strategies, game theory is unavoidably a theory of the formation of preferences among strategies. Although game theorists do not talk about preferences among strategies, there are no grounds to deny that they exist and that game theory shows what they depend on.

5.1. GAMES AND OUTCOMES

Consider the simple extensive "game form" shown in Figure 5.1 with the first number in each pair representing the monetary result for Jill and the second the result for Jack:

Jill moves first and can either play *down*, in which case she gets $4 and Jack gets $2, or Jill can play *across*, in which case Jack gets to play *left* or *right*. If Jack plays *left*, he gets $5 and Jill gets $2. If Jack plays *right*, both receive $4. All of this is common knowledge. Figure 5.1 depicts a "game form," rather than the extensive form of a game, because it does not specify Jack and Jill's preferences. In order to go to work on this strategic interaction, game theorists need to know the player's preferences over the terminal nodes. They need to know not just the *game form* or *game "protocol"* (Weibull 2004), but the *game*. If Jill and Jack are both altruists, they are playing a different game than if they care only about the monetary results for themselves. Game theory requires that preferences over outcomes be given.

Suppose that Jill's and Jack's preferences over the outcomes depend exclusively on their own monetary returns. In that case, the game form shown in Figure 5.1 constitutes the extensive-form *game* shown in Figure 5.2.

Preferences in Positive Economics

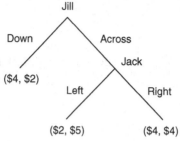

Figure 5.1. A game form.

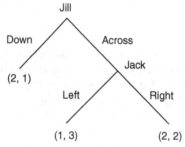

Figure 5.2. A game with this form.

The numbers here are (ordinal) utilities, with larger numbers for alternatives that are more preferred by the individual agent. These numbers are not interpersonally comparable – one should not, for example, conclude that Jack's and Jill's preferences for the outcome of {*across, right*} are equal. These numbers, which drive choices, are supposed to be givens, concerning which economists have nothing to say. If Jack gets to play, he prefers moving *left* rather than *right, because* he prefers the outcome of playing *left* to the outcome of playing *right*. Jill knows this and consequently she prefers to play *down* rather than *across*. Preferences over alternative moves at particular nodes or information sets and hence the preferences over alternative strategies (which are complete specifications of what is chosen at each point where a player gets to act) are explained and predicted from the player's beliefs and their preferences over the outcomes. This explanation is consequentialist.

To define the game, preferences over outcomes must be given, but the game theorist has little to do if the preferences of the players over their strategies are already known. If preferences over strategies are simply given, predicting how players will move is a trivial task. *Game theorists have both an object to study and a task to carry out only if players' preferences over outcomes are given and players' strategy choices (or preferences over strategies) are not given.* Game theory looks as if it were a consequentialist theory of the formation of preferences among strategies on the basis of beliefs and predetermined preferences among outcomes. The asymmetry between preferences among outcomes and preferences among strategies is not always defensible. One reason for this is that the notion of an "outcome" is ambiguous. The numbers at the terminal nodes represent the preferences of the players for what Sen calls "comprehensive outcomes" – that is, following some particular path through the particular extensive form as well as achieving its result. The preference indices attached to the terminal nodes need not match the preferences the players have among the history-less states of affairs that obtain at each terminal node, which Sen calls "culmination outcomes" (1997b, p. 745). Game theorists often assume that these preferences are the same, but they do not need to be. For example, suppose that Jack were the second player in an ultimatum game (in which the first player proposes a division of a sum of money, which the second player can accept or reject. If the proposed split is rejected then both players get nothing.) Jack might reject Jill's proposed $8/$2 split of $10, but Jack might accept the very same division if it were generated by a chance mechanism rather than the decision of another player (Blount 1995). The culmination outcomes (monetary results) are the same, but the comprehensive outcomes are different. In one case Jack might want to punish Jill for making an unfair offer, whereas in the other case, there is no one to punish, and Jack might prefer $2 to nothing. Games are defined by preferences over comprehensive outcomes rather than preferences over culmination outcomes.[1] The (1, 3) at the end of the path {*across, left*} in Figure 5.2 expresses how the players evaluate *everything* about Jill playing *across* and Jack playing *left*, including, but not limited to, the monetary results. By "outcome" I mean "comprehensive outcome." When speaking of what Sen calls "culmination outcomes," I shall talk of "physical results," "monetary results," or simply "results." I take "payoffs" to be preferences over comprehensive outcomes. The fact that the sequence of choices partly *constitutes* the outcome creates complications for consequentialist derivations of preferences over those choices from preferences over outcomes.

An alternative way of making the same point is to insist that the results of the strategic interaction shown in Figure 5.1 are incompletely specified. The result of Jill playing *across* and Jack playing *left* is not a pair of dollar payments. The result consists instead of the state of affairs where in this interaction Jill plays *across*, Jack plays *left*, Jill receives $2, and Jack receives $5. To

---

[1] One might worry about whether normal form representations of games (such as Figure 3.2) provide all the information needed to define comprehensive outcomes. Notice that comprehensive outcomes may depend not only on the results and the path through the game to the results, but also on player's interpretations of why others make the choices that they do. For example, an overly generous offer in an ultimatum game, that is interpreted as a gesture of superiority (as appears to have been the case among Lamalera whalers [Alvard 2004]) may provoke a different response than one that is interpreted as an act of kindness.

define the game, one needs to know the preferences of the players over such fully specified results. This specification of the results must coincide with how the players understand the alternatives they face and their results.

5.2. CONSEQUENTIALISM IN GAME THEORY

The distinction between culmination and comprehensive outcomes – between, in my terminology, results and outcomes – is important, because people may have reasons for preferring paths through game trees, including their own strategies, that do not derive from preferences among the results. In the game form shown in Figure 5.1, Jill might, for example, be more interested in having Jack choose than she is in winning a few dollars more or less. This is a case of what Sen calls "chooser dependence" (1997b, pp. 747–51), and he describes ordinary circumstances where, for reasons of courtesy, people avoid choosing the piece of fruit or the comfortable chair they would prefer if they did not have to choose it. Jill may choose to play across because of her interest in Jack's choosing not because of the monetary results.

Although game theory provides no consequentialist explanation or prediction of Jill's strategy choice, a case such as this one can easily be accommodated. Game theorists can sensibly maintain that if Jill has an overriding desire that Jack choose, then Jill and Jack are not playing the game shown in Figure 5.2. Similar comments apply if Jack prefers to play *right* to reward Jill's apparent trust and benevolence. Notice that it matters how Jack *explains* Jill's *across* move. If Jack thinks that Jill plays *across* out of curiosity, Jack may be less likely to play *right* than if he believes that Jill is playing across because she trusts Jack, or because she wants to be nice. Such considerations do not preclude the possibility of formulating some other consequentialist account of strategy choices, perhaps in terms of characteristics of those choices, but the game theoretic derivations of strategies no longer constitute consequentialist explanations or predictions of them.

If Jill plays across because she wants Jack to have to make a choice, then the utilities in the game shown in Figure 5.2 do not match her preferences over comprehensive outcomes. Because Jill prefers to play *across*, the game theorist must assign a larger utility for Jill to the comprehensive outcomes resulting from her playing *across* than from the outcome of playing *down*. The game theorist will accordingly claim that rather than playing the game shown in Figure 5.2, Jill and Jack are playing the game shown in Figure 5.3.

In Figure 5.3, Jill's preference for playing *across* so that Jack will have to choose has been built into the utilities attached to the terminal nodes.

5.3. THE DEFAULT PRINCIPLE

To apply game theory to interactions among people, economists must decipher people's preferences. To do this, they rely on generalizations about what

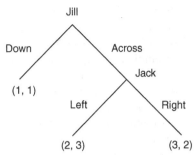

Figure 5.3. Another game with this form.

people's preferences depend on. These generalizations constitute a tacit theory of preference formation. I call the only general principle of this model of preference formation in strategic situations "the default (payoff) principle."

The default principle. Individuals prefer a (comprehensive) *outcome x* to another outcome *y* to exactly the same extent that they prefer the *result* (the "culmination outcome") *x** that *x* involves to the result *y** that *y* involves.

The default principle is only a defeasible presumption. In the interactions presented earlier in the chapter, the results are all monetary, and the default principle can be restated as the claim that players' preferences over outcomes depend exclusively on the monetary facts.

The default principle says only that a player's preferences depend on the physical results for all the players, not that a player's preferences depend exclusively on his or her *own* results. The default principle leaves open the possibility of "pure" altruism or inequity aversion (Fehr and Schmidt 1999), although it rules out as motivations reciprocal altruism, trustworthiness, or what Sen calls "chooser dependence" or "menu dependence." These motivations require more information than merely the culmination results. One reason why economists often prefer to describe non-self-interested preferences as altruistic rather than as trustworthy or reciprocating is that in that way they can continue to uphold the default principle and a consequentialist explanatory and predictive strategy.

The default principle can lead game theorists astray, because other things apart from the results may influence what people do. If a particular strategy involves betraying a trust, a player may reject it for that reason. Some people in Jack's position might, for example, see the little interaction depicted in Figure 5.1 this way and decide to play right in response to Jill's playing across. Some people regard betraying a trust as a relevant feature of a (comprehensive) *outcome*. If economists adjust the utilities they assign to reflect such trustworthiness, then they can continue to relate strategy choices to preferences among comprehensive outcomes, but their derivations will not constitute consequentialist explanations or predictions of those choices.

The default principle is obviously not a universal truth. Preferences over outcomes do not always coincide with preferences over results. There is nothing impossible or irrational about Jack preferring $5 for himself and $2 for someone else to $4 for each in a simple choice, while at the same time preferring to play *right* in the interaction depicted in Figure 5.1 in response to Jill playing *across*. Unless game theorists were able to distinguish preferences over outcomes from preferences over the results, their theory would give false predictions and bad advice. So economists must recognize that the default principle may lead them astray. When the default principle breaks down, consequentialism may not be a useful explanatory or predictive strategy – although by adjusting the payoffs (the preferences of the players over the comprehensive outcomes), economists can continue to appear to conform to it.

The default principle is a fragment of an unacknowledged and largely undeveloped theory of preference formation that economists need to define what games people are playing and to apply game theory. This unacknowledged theory is essential to the application of game theory, but it is not regarded as a part of game theory itself. There are no other general principles in this unacknowledged theory besides the default principle, although there have been proposals for ways to modify the default principle to take account of nonresult features of games that influence preferences over outcomes. Matthew Rabin's (1993) proposal for allowing reciprocation to influence utilities is one example.

Neither the default principle nor modifications of it are a part of what currently constitutes game theory. Game theory takes over only *after* preferences over comprehensive outcomes are specified. Game theory is just one part of a theory of strategic interactions, which presupposes that preferences among comprehensive outcomes have already been determined. An account of what determines preferences among comprehensive outcomes ought also to be a part of economics, but it is not yet a formal or explicitly conceptualized part.

Having specified the game in Figure 5.3, the game theorist can determine which strategies are rationally defensible. The game theorist can point out that *across* dominates *down* for Jill, and Jack then prefers *left* to *right*. There is a unique Nash equilibrium strategy pair, which is derived, in apparent conformity to consequentialism, from preferences over (comprehensive) outcomes. Although Jill may prefer the *result* pair {$4, $2} to {$2, $5}, her preferences among the *outcomes* of the game form in Figure 5.1 are not as the default principle would predict. Instead they reflect Jill's desire that Jack choose.

This analysis of the game shown in Figure 5.3 is entirely orthodox, but game theory is doing very little work. Knowing Jill's preference for playing *across*, the game theorist adjusts the utilities attached to the outcomes so that when it is time to put game theory to work, it implies that Jill plays *across*. In the analysis of the *game*, the game theorist derives the strategy choices from preferences over outcomes, but this turns reality partly on its head. Jill's choice is already determined by her desire that Jack move. This fact can be embedded in the preferences over the comprehensive outcomes so that consequentialism as a principle of rationality is safe. But in this case, the preferences over outcomes are not causally prior to preferences over strategies. These payoffs are given or prior only in the sense that game theory says nothing about the process of assigning them or what they depend on.

The dependence of payoffs on preferences among strategies I have explored in this case is causal rather than epistemic. The reason why in this case preferences over payoffs do not explain preferences over strategies is not that preferences over payoffs cannot be known independently of preferences over strategies. There are, to be sure, epistemic difficulties involved in learning the preferences of players, since one cannot read them off from a player's preferences over the results. But the epistemic difficulties derive from the more fundamental causal complexities. The problems of learning people's preferences and modeling interactions as games, which may be serious, derive from the nonepistemic fact that preferences among outcomes sometimes causally depend on features of game forms other than their results.

When the default principle holds, the structure of the explanations, predictions, and advice game theory offers is unproblematic, as are the possibilities of applying game theory. Preferences over outcomes are causally prior to preferences over strategies, and game theory provides an account of strategy choice that is consequentialist in both form and reality. Since there are significant domains where the default principle holds, game theory has important applications. But when the default principle does not hold, preferences over outcomes have to be determined before game theory can take over and treat them as exogenous – and thereby provide the appearance of a consequentialist determination of strategy choices.

5.4. CONCLUSIONS: THE CONSEQUENCES OF CONSEQUENTIALISM

The accepted view that preferences are the "given" starting point about which economics has and should have nothing to say is misleading both with respect to circumstances in which the default principle holds (and preferences over outcomes are given) and with respect to circumstances in which the default principle is mistaken and preferences over outcomes have to be determined. When the default principle holds, game theory and, *a fortiori*, expected-utility theory can function as theories that explain preferences over gambles or over strategies in terms of prior preferences over their results. When the default principle fails, then the conventional view of expected-utility theory as merely representing preferences may seem more justified, because there is no simple causal story whereby preferences over the immediate objects of choice are derived from preferences over their consequences and subjective probabilities. But at the same time, there is another activity (for which there is no explicit theory) that derives preferences over comprehensive outcomes from the many different reasons people have for preferring strategies, actions, and results.

In either case, to provide a nontrivial model that predicts choices, explains choices, or offers advice on choices, economists must show what the preferences for those choices depend on and thus must provide a theory of the formation of those preferences. Consequentialism provides one structure within which economists fill out the agent's preferences. This is the structure employed by the standard model, and when the default principle holds, consequentialist accounts are straightforward. When the default principle does not hold, game theory and expected-utility theory still need to link preferences among alternative actions to preferences among their properties and consequences. But without the empirical determinacy provided by the default principle, these connections may fail to provide a nontrivial prediction or explanation of choice.

Although the only account of preference formation that shows up explicitly within game theory is the account of how preferences over strategies depend on preferences over outcomes and the structure of the interaction, those interested in strategic interactions also need to understand what shapes preferences over comprehensive outcomes. That understanding is a task for economists. Game theory is an important part of the theory of strategic interactions, but it is only a part; economists must also tackle questions concerning preference formation.

6

Constraints and Counterpreferential Choice

In Chapters 4 and 5, I developed a view of consequentialist explanation and prediction that relies on a notion of preferences as total subjective comparative evaluations – rankings that reflect all relevant evaluative considerations and combine with beliefs to determine choices. This view of preferences and of their role in explanation and prediction dominates the practice of mainstream economics. Consequentialism is a sensible explanatory and predictive strategy.

In this approach to explanation and prediction, the panoply of factors that influence people's actions – their plans and passions, their whims and wishes, their tastes and temptations – must all find their place *within* an agent's preferences and beliefs. I have maintained that this is the way that economists understand choices and that it is a reasonable way to proceed.

Amartya Sen disagrees. He argues that it is better not to squeeze everything relevant to action into beliefs and preferences. In addressing Sen's critique, I shall not argue that economists have hit on the only sensible way to study human behavior. There are other ways to parse the factors that influence choices, which have their advantages. Economists have developed one good way to explain and predict behavior, but it is not the only good way. Moreover, this defense of the overall strategy that economists employ comes with qualifications, to which I return in Part III. In particular, I argue that economists should say more about how preferences are formed and modified.

6.1. SYMPATHY AND COMMITMENT

Sen is critical of "the common tendency to make 'preference' (or a general-purpose 'utility function') an all-embracing depository of a person's feelings, values, priorities, choices, and a great many other essentially diverse objects"

(1991a, p. 589). He sees this practice as a conflation of different concepts of preference and as a failure to draw necessary distinctions:

> A person is given *one* preference ordering, and as and when the need arises this is supposed to reflect his interests, represent his welfare, summarize his idea of what should be done, and describe his actual choices and behavior. Can one preference ordering do all these things? A person thus described may be "rational" in the limited sense of revealing no inconsistencies in his choice behavior, but if he has no use for these distinctions between quite different concepts, he must be a bit of a fool. (Sen 1977, pp. 335–36)

Setting aside questions about welfare, to which I return in Chapter 7, what is wrong with employing a single ranking to reflect an agent's interests, summarize the agent's idea of what should be done, and to predict and explain what the agent does?

Sen is impressed with the variety of factors that influence choices and the variety of choices people make. No single set of considerations explains why people may be cutthroats at work, devoted parents at home, liberals at the voting booth, racists at the club, public-spirited at one moment, pious at another, principled before lunch, selfish in the afternoon, and malevolent after dinner. To account for a reasonable portion of human behavior, economists should, Sen maintains, at the very least recognize the existence of what he calls "sympathy" and "commitment." Sympathy obtains when "the concern for others directly affects one's own welfare" (1977, p. 326). Sympathy and expected benefit are thus compatible. Acting out of sympathy (as understood by Sen) involves no self-sacrifice. Commitment in contrast is nonegoistic (1977, pp. 326–27) and *contrary to preference* (at least in the sense of expected advantage) (1977, p. 327). "If knowledge of torture of others makes you sick, it is a case of sympathy; if it does not make you feel personally worse off, but you think it is wrong and you are ready to do something to stop it, it is a case of commitment" (Sen 1977, p. 326).

Sympathy is the way in which benefits and harms to other people register within self-interested preferences. It arises from the fact that many of the sources of expected advantage are states of affairs involving other people. Sympathy is not always positive. Jack may be happier when his friend, Jill, is succeeding in her ambitions, but he may also be miserable when his rival, Zachary, is thriving. When anticipation of this happiness or misery influences Jack's preferences, his preferences are influenced by what Sen calls "sympathy." Recognizing the existence of sympathy in Sen's sense enables one to square behavior that aims to help or harm others with a model of individuals as governed entirely by a concern for their own advantage.

An action that is not motivated by an expectation of benefit and that aims at anything else, including benefitting or harming another person, counts as what Sen calls "commitment" rather than sympathy. Sympathy is thus not altruistic. If Jill's doing *x* is a case of sympathy, she must be motivated by an expectation that she will benefit from doing *x*. Sometimes Jill can expect to benefit from an action, although that expectation is not what motivates her (1977, p. 327). In that case, she is acting out of commitment. She would still have performed the action if she had not expected any benefit for herself. What distinguishes sympathy and commitment is what motivates the action. Commitment, like sympathy, is not always positive. Both altruism and malevolence involve commitment.

If, as I have urged, one takes preferences to be total subjective comparative evaluations, then whatever influences Jill's choices other than constraints and beliefs must do so via her preferences. If economists take preferences to be total rankings and to determine choices, then choice cannot be counterpreferential. Taking commitments to be in accord with preferences (construed as total subjective rankings) does not collapse the distinction between sympathy and commitment. Acting on one's preferences has no implications concerning the content of one's preferences. For example, suppose Jill gives $150 to charity rather than buy an iPod for herself. If her action is in accord with her preferences, then she prefers to make the donation. But her preference does not imply that she expects to benefit more from the donation than from the iPod. She might be motivated by expected benefit if, for example, she anticipates greater happiness from thinking about the good her donation will do than from listening to music. In that case, her action is a case of sympathy. But what motivates her might have no reference to her own interests. In that case, her donation – although, like all intentional actions, consonant with her preferences – would constitute an instance of commitment. The fact that committed actions, like all actions, accord with preference (as a total ranking) does not imply that they aim at the agent's own benefit.

Sen's examples suggest that commitment involves adherence to principle, and it is easy mistakenly to assimilate Sen's distinction between sympathy and commitment to the contrast between action motivated by concerns for others and action motivated by adherence to principle (but see Anderson 2001, p. 22f). This assimilation is mistaken, both because Sen maintains that sympathy must be motivated by an expected benefit to the chooser, and because Sen never explicitly restricts what he calls "commitment" to cases where principles govern choice. Whether or not he means to restrict commitment to acting from principle, Sen defines commitment to include *any* non-self-interested motivation.

6.2. COMMITMENT AND COUNTERPREFERENTIAL CHOICE

In later works, Sen defends the possibility of counterpreferential choice in a stronger sense. He distinguishes three theses whose conjunction leads to the identification of people's preferences with an exclusive concern with their own advantage:

1. "self-centered welfare" (the person's welfare does not depend on benefits or harms to others);

2. "self-welfare goal" (a person's preferences among alternatives depend only on their expected upshot for the person's welfare);
3. "self-goal choice" (a person's choices depend only on his or her own goals). (1985a, pp. 213–14; 1987a, p. 80)

Sen then employs these distinctions in the following remarks:

Sympathy does, specifically, violate self-centered welfare, but commitment does not have such a unique interpretation. It can, of course, reflect the denial of self-welfare goal, and indeed it is perhaps plausible to interpret in this way the example of a person acting to remove the misery of others from which he does not suffer himself. But commitment can also involve violation of self-goal choice, *since the departure may possibly arise from self-imposed restrictions on the pursuit of one's own goals (in favor of, say, following particular rules of conduct)*. (1985a, p. 214 [emphasis added])

When Jack's commitment conflicts only with self-welfare goal, then Jack's choice is still determined by his own preferences. It is just that Jack's preferences are not always addressed to his own advantage. But when commitment conflicts with "self-goal choice," Jack's self-imposed "restrictions on the pursuit of [his] own goals" lead to choice of an option that does not best fulfill his goals. This is a far stronger conception of counterpreferential choice.

Sen uses the word "goals" rather than "preferences," and goals are not the same thing as preferences. For example, unlike preferences, goals are not necessarily comparative. So it might be wrong to take Sen to be arguing that commitment can lead to choices that conflict with preferences, understood as total subjective rankings. If by "goals" Sen means to refer merely to some subset of the factors that determine total rankings, then the "self-imposed restrictions on the pursuit of one's own goals (in favor of, say, following particular rules of conduct)" could be interpreted as other influences on preferences. But Sen takes goals to encompass an extremely wide range of considerations. For example, he writes of goals as "including moral objectives" (1987a, p. 81). For the purposes of this inquiry, let us take Sen as arguing that commitment can lead to actions that conflict with preferences, understood as total comparative evaluations. The following discussion of his arguments supports this interpretation.

6.3. CONSTRAINTS AND COUNTERPREFERENTIAL CHOICE

How could Jack's rational choice be contrary to his total subjective ranking? Should economists make room for counterpreferential choice in their explanatory and predictive models? Sen answers the first question by arguing that commitments can constrain choices in the same way that physical facts do. Jack might not choose x even though he prefers it to y, because he has excluded x from the set of alternatives from which he can choose.

Sen gives an example of his closing the shade on an airplane window so that someone sitting next to him can play a silly computer game. He writes:

How do you explain your choice? There is no difficulty in understanding that you are not averse to helping your neighbour – or anyone else – pursue his or her *well-being*, but it so happens that you do not think that your neighbour's well-being is, in fact, best advanced by his wasting his time – or by your helping him to waste his time – on a silly game. (Sen 2007, pp. 348–49)

But the violation of self-goal choice is arising here from the normative restraints we may voluntarily impose on ourselves on grounds of recognising other people's pursuits and goals, without in any substantive sense making them our own goals. (2007, pp. 353–54)

Sen's thought is that self-imposed constraints can create a gulf between what Jack prefers and what he does. He argues that economists should model self-imposed constraints this way rather than including them among the factors that determine preferences, because self-imposed constraints influence choice in a different way than do desires, aversions, whims or wishes. Modeling commitments as literally constraints permits economists to capture the distinction between those things people do (or don't do) because of their preferences and those things they rule out, regardless of what they would like. For example, consider the reasons why people do not commit crimes. Sometimes they simply prefer not to. An accomplished pickpocket who has no scruples about theft may be flush at the moment or feel sorry for a potential victim and so pass up an easy snatch. In other cases, people refuse even to consider committing crimes. When he sees a wad of bills falling out of a fellow bus-rider's jacket pocket, it never even occurs to Jack to swipe it, however much Jack might need the money and however low he might estimate the odds of getting caught. Stealing is not an option. This distinction is tacitly recognized by economists, who define the budget set in most models of consumer choice theory as including only those bundles of commodities people can purchase, not also those that they can steal. Since stealing is not impossible, this constraint on the budget set is partly self-imposed. Constraints rule out certain alternatives rather than increasing or decreasing the weight of considerations for or against them. This advantage of treating self-imposed constraints separately from factors influencing preferences is not decisive, because self-imposed constraints are not inviolable, and something needs to be said about how agents decide when they should violate them.

Sen's proposal to make room for counterpreferential choice that derives from self-imposed constraints faces two significant difficulties. First, the notion of a constraint on choice that is self-imposed merely by an act of will seems paradoxical. Sometimes people impose constraints on their actions by creating objective barriers to certain choices, as in the case of those who commit themselves to an institution in order to bring an addiction under control. But what Sen has in mind is a purely psychological constraint: An individual simply rules out certain alternatives. Having ruled out some alternatives, Jack knows that nothing other than his own will is preventing him from choosing them. How then can Jack believe that the excluded alternatives *cannot* be chosen? Would it not be more straightforward to model self-imposed constraints as features of preferences? As Bratman (1987, pp. 5f) shows, this objection – which can also be directed toward theories of intentions – can be met, but not if one models behavior as determined by constraints, beliefs, and preferences.

Second, and more seriously, interpreting commitment as self-imposed constraint does not show how counterpreferential choice is possible. It shows only how choices might misleadingly appear to be counterpreferential. For example, Jill sees Sen lower his airplane window shade, although she knows that he would prefer to leave it open, and concludes that Sen's action violates self-goal choice. But given the constraints he has imposed on which alternatives are available for choice, in fact he chooses what he most prefers. The case is like one where Jack jumps out of a window, even though he would prefer to remain safely in his apartment, because a fire rules out the possibility of remaining safely in his apartment or leaving via the stairs. Among the feasible alternatives – jumping or succumbing to smoke inhalation – Jack chooses what he most prefers. Similarly, if Sen's acceptance of norms of courtesy rules out the possibility that he can leave his shade open, then closing it does not violate self-goal choice. It appears to Jill to do so because she has misidentified the set of feasible alternatives.

There is no way to make sense of counterpreferential choice without rejecting the interpretation of preferences as total comparative evaluations. The standard model of choice permits one to model commitments as influencing choices via influencing preferences or to model them as Sen suggests as changing the constraints. I think it is generally simpler and more straightforward to take commitments to be as among the factors that determine preferences.

6.4. MANY CONCEPTS OF PREFERENCE OR JUST ONE?

Sen's underlying concern is to push economists toward a more nuanced view of rational choice (see particularly his 1985b and the introduction to his 2002). He criticizes a view of decision makers as rational fools who carry around some set of final preferences among the feasible alternatives that match their view of expected benefit, and simply choose an alternative at the top of the ranking. Alan Gibbard makes a similar point:

If we try to use preferences as a psychological, explanatory notion, the decision theorist's characterization may not do very well. Motivations are of diverse kinds. They can be grounded in emotions, in craving and appetites, in the maintenance of self-esteem, in the social pressures of one's circumstances, and in the acceptance of norms. A good psychology of human motivation would presumably extend this list and revise it. (1998, p. 250)

Economists should recognize that there are many different ways in which alternatives are valued and hence, Sen maintains, many different conceptions of preference.

Those who believe, as I do, that economists should employ a single notion of preference as a total subjective comparative evaluation might disagree with Sen either about how nuanced human motivation is or about how to model motivational complexity. Some economists have maintained that people are not so complicated or that economists can safely ignore the complications. Although there are few people who care for nothing apart from wealth, many economists have maintained that in some domains people's choices are, to a high degree of approximation, governed by some single evaluative consideration, such as expected monetary gain. One response to Sen is thus to maintain that people are rational fools.

This is not my view. I agree with Sen that human motivation is very complicated, but I disagree with him about how it should be modeled. Rather than capturing this complexity by means of multiple concepts of preference or by not theorizing in terms of preference, I suggest that economists should provide nuanced accounts of some of the factors that influence preferences. People prefer some things because of their expected benefits, others because of specific properties, others because of emotional reactions toward other people, others because of adherence to social norms or to moral principles, others out of mere habit. Depending on the context and the objectives, the factors that influence preferences can be simple or complicated. The mere reliance on a complete, transitive, and stable ranking of alternatives does not make someone a rational fool. If that ranking is properly sensitive to all relevant evaluative criteria, then it will result in sensible rather than foolish action. In my view, the considerations that drive Sen to insist on the multiplicity of notions of preference instead justify identifying preferences with total subjective rankings while at the same time distinguishing sharply between preferences on the one hand and, on the other hand, expected advantage, moral commitments, or any other substantive dimension of evaluation.

Many economists would go on to argue for a division of labor, whereby psychologists, sociologists, and philosophers study how people form and modify their total subjective rankings, and economists investigate the consequences of the choices that arise from those rankings when combined with expectations and constraints. But taking preferences to be total rankings does not imply that economists should not be concerned about how such rankings are constructed and changed. To attribute to people a total subjective ranking of alternatives is a strong idealization, which will be unreasonable in many contexts. Without thinking about where this ranking comes from, economists will not understand when such an idealization is sensible and when it is not. Nor will they understand how changing beliefs and circumstances will influence both preferences and action. As Sen has shown – albeit in other terminology – the task of understanding how agents construct and modify their preferences should not be left out of economics.

In addition to the expected advantage and choice construals of preferences, Sen claims that economists have taken preferences to refer to "mental satisfaction," "desires," and "values" (1997a, p. 303).[1] Sen goes on to argue that "the eschewal of these distinctions in the characterization of persons amounts to seeing people as 'rational fools,' as undiscriminating and gross thinkers, who choose one all-purpose preference order.... A theory of human behaviour – even on economic matters – calls for much more structure and many more distinctions" (1997a, p. 304).

Sen is right to maintain that "[a] theory of human behaviour – even on economic matters – calls for much more structure and many more distinctions." It does not follow, however, that it needs multiple notions of *preference*. Sen's concern to discriminate among the many factors that influence choices can be accommodated at least as well by distinguishing sharply *between* preferences (as total subjective comparative evaluations) and the many things that shape preferences. Malice, benevolence, and self-interest are three important human motivations. Rather than taking them to be concepts of preference, one can distinguish *between*, on the one hand, wanting to harm others, wanting to benefit them, and wanting to benefit oneself and, on the other hand, preferences that result from weighing these wants and other considerations. A theory purporting to explain or predict the ways in which agents evaluate states of affairs needs to discriminate between, for example, values and mere tastes, long-run plans and internalized norms, or between reciprocal altruism and trust. These should be seen as distinctions among the factors that are responsible for a person's preferences, not as different conceptions of preference.

Those who take preference to be a total subjective ranking can in this way accommodate Sen's concern with the complexities of rational choice. But why is it better to accept a single conception of preferences as total comparative evaluations (as I maintain) rather than recognizing many conceptions, as Sen urges? Does it matter whether economists take "preferences" to be multiply ambiguous or whether instead they take "preferences" to be total subjective rankings and give other names to what Sen takes to be other conceptions of preference?

There are four reasons why economists should reject Sen's advice and instead adopt a single notion of preference as a total comparative evaluation. First, to regard choice rankings, expected advantage rankings, hypothetical choice rankings, "mental satisfaction," "values," "tastes," "all motivational considerations other than principle," and "total subjective rankings" as eight different conceptions of preference is an invitation to perpetuate the confusions that Sen has criticized. To mark the distinctions between these different things, economists should use different words. The justification for retaining the word "preference" for the last of these eight concepts is that it matches economic practice.

---

[1] And utility, which is frequently taken to be an index of preference, has an even wider range of meanings. See Sen 1987b, pp. 5–7, and Sen 1991b.

Second, regarding these rankings as alternative conceptions of preference makes it difficult to pose questions concerning what things determine preferences. The concept of a total subjective comparative evaluation is the most suitable concept of preference, precisely because it does not settle *a priori* what influences preferences. By treating preferences as total rankings, economists can separate the use of the word "preference" from substantive views about what preferences depend on.

Third, some of the supposed conceptions of "preference" fly in the face of everyday understandings of the word.[2] Everyday usage is not determinative, and indeed the interpretation of preferences in economics that I defend conflicts with everyday usage. But conforming roughly to everyday usage helps avoid misunderstandings. Taking preferences to imply total comparative evaluations modestly extends the everyday notion of preferences (as overall comparative evaluations) in a way that serves the purposes of economists and decision theorists.

Finally, as I argue in the next section, only the conception of preferences as total subjective comparative evaluations permits game theory and expected-utility theory to serve their predictive and explanatory roles.

6.5. GAME THEORY AND COUNTERPREFERENTIAL CHOICE

Sometimes rational choice, as understood in economics, appears to be truly foolish. Sen maintains (wrongly, in my view) that one of those contexts is the prisoner's dilemma game, which has, he argues, a more reasonable interpretation if one refuses to build all evaluative considerations into preferences. In examining this case, one can better understand Sen's position and how his concerns can be accommodated by the univocal view of preferences I have defended.

Consider the interaction whose normal form is shown in Figure 6.1. The first number indicates the dollar payoff to the row player (Jill) from each strategy combination and the second the dollar payoff to the column player (Jack).

Assume that the game form is common knowledge. Each player correctly expects to earn a larger monetary payoff by playing strategy D "defect" than by playing strategy C ("cooperate"), regardless of what the other player does. (The players choose simultaneously – without knowing what the other player does – and neither can influence the choice of the other.) Yet both wind up with less money if both play D than if both play C. Figure 6.1 does *not* depict a game. By definition, economists have not specified a game until they have assigned preferences to the outcomes.

---

[2] This claim requires qualification, because many people believe that people's preferences are always dictated by their self-interest, and many hold the psychological hedonist view that whatever people do, they do because of the pleasure they expect. But these mistaken views of preference depend on well-known philosophical mistakes. There is no virtue in following ordinary usage when ordinary usage is confused.

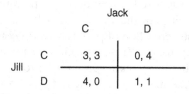

Figure 6.1. A prisoner's dilemma game form.

Jack

		C	D
	C	3, 3	0, 4
Jill			
	D	4, 0	1, 1

Figure 6.2. A prisoner's dilemma game.

If in addition each player cares only about his or her own financial payoff, and this is common knowledge, then one has the prisoner's dilemma game shown in Figure 6.2.

Figure 6.2 is the normal form of a game of complete information. In games of complete information, the strategy choices, the outcomes, and the player's preferences (utilities) are common knowledge. D is a strictly dominant strategy for both players – that is, whatever choice the other player makes, each does better playing D rather than C. But both do worse if both play D than if both play C.

Many people mistakenly believe that this result is paradoxical.[3] "How can it be rational to play D, if both do better by playing C?" Many people thus

---

[3] In contrast, the analysis of finitely iterated prisoner's dilemmas or centipede games employing backward induction leads to arguably irrational recommendations. As an illustration of a centipede interaction, suppose there is $4 in the middle of the table. The first player, Jack, can either take three-fourth of the pot ($3) leaving $1 for the second player, Mary, or pass. If Jack takes the $3, the game ends. If a player passes, the money on the table is doubled. In the second round, Mary can take $6 and leave $2 for Jack or pass, and in the third round, Jack can take $12 and leave $4 for Mary or pass. The game ends after ten rounds. If, in the last round, with $2,048 in the pot, Mary does not take three-fourth for herself, then the money is divided evenly:

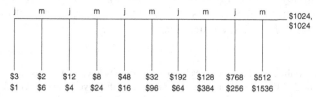

If Mary gets to decide between taking three-fourth of the $2,048 or dividing it equally and she cares only about her own dollar payoffs, Mary will take three-fourth of the $2,048, leaving

maintain that it is rational to play C rather than D and that experimental subjects, who often in fact play cooperatively, have the last laugh on the supposedly oh-so-rational game theorists. But notice that the reason why Jack does better if both he and Jill play C than if they both play D is that he benefits from Jill's choosing C. Choosing to play C himself always leads to a worse outcome in terms of his own preferences. Since this is a one-shot game in which there is no role for reputation or reciprocation and no way to influence what the other does, Jack and Jill always harm themselves while benefitting the other if they play C. If the indices correctly indicate their total rankings of outcomes, then each should play D. Their misfortune lies in being paired with each other in an interaction structured this way.

All of this is uncontroversial if the utility numbers represent total subjective comparative evaluations of the comprehensive outcomes. Call this "the orthodox interpretation" of game theory. If utilities represent total rankings, then individuals who play C when faced with the game form in Figure 6.1 are either irrational or their preferences do not depend only on their own monetary payoff (Binmore 1994). By taking utilities to represent total subjective comparative evaluations, game theorists are able to predict and explain strategy choices in terms of facts about games, including rankings of their outcomes. Outcomes are "comprehensive" rather than "cumulative" (see Section 5.1), because players may care about features of the path through the game tree in addition to its culmination.

This orthodox interpretation of the utility payoffs in game theory limits game theory proper to an examination of how strategy choices depend on game forms, beliefs, and total rankings of comprehensive outcomes. How individuals construct their total comparative evaluations of comprehensive outcomes is not a part of game theory. When faced with the fact that experimenters find high rates of cooperation in interactions that appear to have the structure of prisoner's dilemmas, all the game theorist can say is that the subjects are irrational or, more plausibly, that their preferences do not depend only on their own monetary payoff and hence that the subjects are not playing a prisoner's dilemma game after all. If the subjects who play strategy C are rational, then, in terms of their own total evaluation of outcomes, D cannot be a dominant strategy. But the game theorist has nothing to say about how individuals think about their strategic interactions and how they decide how

---

Jack with $512, so Jack (who also cares only about his own monetary payoff) is better off taking three-fourth of the $1,024 pot in the ninth round, and Mary is better off taking three-fourth of the $512 pot on the eighth round. Iterating this reasoning – that is, applying backward induction – the rational thing for Jack to do is to take $3 in the first round and end the game. That seems just plain dumb. If Jack does not take $3 in the first round, why should Mary end the game in the second round by taking $6 (three-fourth of the $8 pot) to forestall the possibility that Jack will end the game in the third round and leave her with only $4? It would be wise to do so only if Mary is confident that Jack will end the game in the third round, but since he did not end the game in the first round, why should she be confident that he will end the game in the third round?

to rank comprehensive outcomes. The task resides instead in a sort of limbo. Economists have not formally addressed it (although, with the development of behavioral economics, that may be changing), and it is scarcely studied by any other discipline either.

If one thinks of preferences as Sen does, as not exhausting all of the factors that may be relevant to choice, then it is possible for agents rationally to choose one strategy even though they "prefer" the outcomes of another. For example, suppose the utilities in Figure 6.2 indicated a *partial* ranking in terms of expected advantage rather than a total ranking. If other considerations apart from expected advantage influence choice, then this interpretation of the payoffs makes room for counterpreferential rational choice. The fact that D is a dominant strategy in terms of expected advantage does not imply that rational individuals will play D. One opens a space in which to discuss the thought processes that may lead individuals to make choices that are not governed by their expected advantage. So there may be a significant gain in interpreting preferences more narrowly than as total comparative evaluations.

Sen's argument that cooperation can be rational in one-shot prisoner's dilemmas does not rest on interpreting preferences in terms of expected advantage. Indeed he notes that altruists whose preferences conflict with expected advantage can find themselves in a prisoner's dilemma, too. Regardless of the specific interpretation of preferences, Sen's approach requires that they not incorporate all of the considerations bearing on choice. Sen writes:

> The language of game theory ... makes it ... very tempting to think that whatever a person may appear to be maximizing, on a simple interpretation, must be that person's goal.... There is a genuine ambiguity here when the instrumental value of certain *social* rules are accepted for the *general* pursuit of *individual* goals. If reciprocity is not taken to be intrinsically important, but instrumentally so, and that recognition is given expression in actual reciprocal behaviour, for achieving each person's own goals better, it is hard to argue that the person's "real goal" is to follow reciprocity rather than their respective actual goals. (1987a, pp. 85–86)

I interpret these complicated remarks as follows: Suppose the utilities that define a prisoner's dilemma game reflect only *intrinsic* evaluative considerations. They are not influenced by considerations concerning trustworthiness, reciprocity, and other factors that do not show up in the culmination outcomes. If the player's actions are influenced by considerations such as reciprocity or trustworthiness, then it can be rational for them to play C, despite the fact that C is dominated in terms of intrinsic considerations. As Sen maintains, when the reciprocity the players show is instrumental to pursuit of what they value intrinsically, "it is hard to argue that the person's 'real goal' [or preference] is to follow reciprocity rather than their respective actual goals."

Sen is right about the importance of modeling the intricate thought processes individuals go through when faced with strategic problems like the one shown in Figure 6.1, and his suggestion that those who decide to cooperate may still in some sense "prefer" the results where they defect to the results where they cooperate is plausible. Sen's approach permits one to model a wider range of the thought processes that lead to actions in strategic situations such as shown in Figure 6.1 than do the standard game-theoretical treatments.

When one asks game theorists why so many individuals facing the situation shown in Figure 6.1 cooperate, they should have something better to say than, "That's not our department. Go talk to the social psychologists." Sen's proposal that economists adopt a multiplicity of notions of preference corresponding to different specific evaluative concerns and interpret the payoffs of games so that strategy choices are no longer deducible from normal forms such as the one shown in Figure 6.2 is one way to address the complexities of the players' interpretations of the strategic situation. I maintain, however, that the costs of divorcing choice from preference and belief are too high. If preference and belief do not determine choice, what will? Preserving the possibility of predicting what players will choose from the specification of the game they are playing provides a decisive reason to take preferences to be total rankings.

A better way to meet Sen's concerns is to conclude that economists need more than game theory and preference-based prediction and explanation. To model strategic interactions, they also need to investigate how players construct their preferences over comprehensive outcomes. Modeling the process whereby people construct games from the parameters of strategic situations is not easy. But it can be done. For example, Cristina Bicchieri has recently proposed a formal model that incorporates social norms into the preferences of agents (2005, pp. 52–53). A strategy profile renders a norm applicable to an individual j (in Bicchieri's terms, "instantiates" a norm for j) if there is a norm specifying what j should do in the game given the strategies that the others actually follow. A strategy profile violates a norm if for at least one player j there is a norm applicable to j that j does not obey. Bicchieri's norm-inclusive utility function is as follows:

$$U_j(s) = \pi_j(s) - k_j \pi_{ml}(s).$$

I have changed some of her notation to one that I find easier to interpret. $\pi_j(s)$ is what j's payoff would be in the game, if j were not influenced by any social norms. k_j a number that reflects how sensitive j is to the relevant social norm. $\pi_{ml}(s)$ is the maximum loss to any individual resulting from any norm violations by individual strategies in the strategy profile s, but never less than zero. How badly someone violates a norm is measured by the maximum impact the norm violation has on any player's preferences. If there is no loss to the norm violation or no norm violation, then $U_j(s) = \pi_j(s)$. k_j is specific to the particular agent and situation. Agents may be intensely concerned to adhere to some norms in some situations and unconcerned to adhere to norms in other situations.

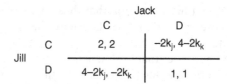

Figure 6.3. A prisoner's dilemma with social norms.

To illustrate how this is supposed to work, suppose there is a social norm calling for cooperation in the prisoner's dilemma depicted in Figure 6.2. If both play C, then the second term in Bicchieri's utility function for both is zero, and so the payoff for the strategy pair {C, C} is unchanged. If Jill plays C and Jack violates the norm and plays D, then Jill's utility is $0 - 2k_j$ and Jack's is $4 - 2k_k$. Similarly, if Jill plays D and Jack plays C, Jill's utility is $4 - 2k_j$ and Jack's is $0 - 2k_k$. Because no norms are applicable to Jack or Jill when both play D, the payoffs to the strategy pair {D, D} are unchanged. So the actual payoffs in the game Jill and Jack are playing are as shown in Figure 6.3. If both k_j and k_k are greater than or equal to one, then this is a coordination game in which cooperation is rational.[4]

I do not mean to defend Bicchieri's proposal, the details of which I have criticized elsewhere (Hausman 2008a). I have discussed it only to illustrate how economists might accommodate Sen's concerns without surrendering the view of preferences as total rankings. To argue that economists should seek an explicit theory of how games are constituted, which would include an account of how individuals in a strategic interaction construct their beliefs and preferences, does not require that economists break the connection between dominant strategies and rational choices. The way to win Sen's battle – and I see myself as his ally, not his opponent – is for economists to model the process of interpreting strategic circumstances as games, rather than to reconceptualize games, which is what rejecting the concept of preferences as total subjective comparative evaluations requires.

---

[4] For example, suppose that k_j and k_k were both equal to 2. Then they would be playing the following game:

		Jack	
		C	D
Jill	C	2, 2	–4, 0
	D	0, –4	1, 1

Each prefers a strategy if and only if the other chooses the same strategy. If both play C, both are better off than if both play D, but it is also safer to play D in the sense that if the players fail to coordinate, the payoff to D is 0, whereas the payoff to C is –4.

6.6. COMMITMENTS AND INTENTIONS

I have argued that economists should adhere to a single conception of preferences as total subjective comparative evaluations. In that way they avoid confusion, clearly locate questions about the specific factors that drive choice (via their influence on preferences), and make unambiguous predictions concerning choices. Given their goals, they have hit on the right conception of preferences, even if, in their reflections on their practice, they may have misdescribed their own concept.

There are many questions to be asked about human action, and models that begin with a complete preference ranking are a good way to answer only some of them. For example, if one is interested in how features of the choice situation influence evaluations, then it is not helpful to suppose that all the evaluations have already been accomplished.

Models of action in terms of preferences, beliefs, and constraints are also not appropriate tools to respond to many of the hard questions philosophers have asked. (See, for example, Bratman 1987, 1999, 2007a; Danto 1973; Davidson 1980, 2004; Dretske 1991; En 2006; Mele 1997; Pietrofski 2000; Schroeder 2007; Schapiro 2009; or Tuomela 1977). For instance, what is the difference between embracing a desire and repudiating a desire? If preferences are already settled, this question will never come up. What is it to be an agent? How should self-governance be understood? What are intentions and how are they related to preferences? How should one understand "weakness of will," whereby people make choices that are inconsistent with their settled desires?

The fact that models in which preferences are already given or have a consequentialist derivation will not help with many of the questions philosophers ask does not refute the standard model of choice. The fact that it is unhelpful for some purposes to pass over the complexities of human agency, including the roles of intention and self-governance, does not imply that models that pass over these complexities are not useful for other purposes. Models that explain and predict choices in terms of constraints, beliefs, and total comparative evaluations do not deny that human agency and motivation are complicated matters. They instead locate those complications in theories of preference formation and modification rather than in theories of choice. Because these complications are important and relevant to their explanatory and predictive concerns, economists need to model preference formation, but the fact that their accounts of the relations between preferences, beliefs, and choices do not serve the purposes of psychologists and philosophers does not imply that they need to abandon their modeling strategy.

In arguing that commitment, as counterpreferential choice, is precluded by a notion of preferences as total comparative evaluations, I argued that commitment should be understood as one of the factors determining total evaluations rather than as competing with preferences. I did not argue that commitment is not real or important. On the contrary, I believe that a notion of commitment much like Sen's has a crucial role to play in understanding agency. Consider Michael Bratman's striking discussion of eight hypothetical "creatures" with increasingly sophisticated deliberative capacities (2007b, pp. 51–61).

Creature 1 acts on its strongest desire at time of action.

Creature 2 acts on its beliefs and considered desires.

Creature 3 can deliberate in face of conflicting desires, whose weights correspond to motivational strength.

Creature 4 can settle in advance on a partial plan of action.

Creature 5 can cope with temptation, and can be motivated by anticipated future regret.

Creature 6 has higher-order desires: It can ask itself whether it wants a given desire to play a particular role in its agency.

Creature 7 can embrace or reject its desires. It is capable of planning and ordering its desires into a hierarchy.

Creature 8 has "the capacity to arrive at policies that express its commitment to being motivated by a desire *by way of its treatment of that desire as providing, in deliberation, a justifying end for action*" (emphasis in the original).

Without the capacity to "deliberate in face of conflicting desires," it is questionable whether creatures 1 and 2 can have preferences. All of the remaining creatures could have complete, transitive, and choice-determining preferences, even though, as I argued in Chapter 2, it is extremely unlikely that the first few creatures could achieve such preferences. The agents in economic models implicitly possess the capacities of at least creature 5.

Commitment in the sense of preferences that conflict with judgments of expected benefit could be present in any of the creatures. Self-imposed constraints, on the other hand, enter at the level of creatures 4 and 5, when a chooser is capable of forming a plan or intention (creature 4) and of sticking to it in the face of conflicting desires (creature 5). As Sen wisely points out, choosers like creatures 1, 2, and 3 are rational fools, and any acceptable philosophical account of agency had better make room for the sort of distinctions that Bratman insightfully introduces. But assigning to agents preference rankings that satisfy the basic axioms and then explaining and predicting behavior in terms of constraints, beliefs, and those preferences does not commit economists to any specific view of agency.

6.7. CONCLUSIONS

This chapter defends the standard model of choice against Sen's criticism that its notion of preference rules out the possibility of making further distinctions of the sort that Sen and Bratman discuss. Although the standard model of choice does not draw the distinctions that Sen and Bratman draw, it does not rule them out. It instead "relocates" concerns about commitments, intentions, self-governance, and so forth to inquiries concerning the determinants of preferences and constraints. In some cases, what is of interest is the complicated interplay between desires, intention, self-command, and so forth, and the determination of actions by the beliefs and preferences of agents is of little interest. In such cases, the standard model of choice is uninformative. In other cases, what is of interest will be the relations between preferences and beliefs and the actions that result from them, although something will still need to be said about what determines final preferences.

Although the last three chapters have deflected philosophical criticisms of the standard model of choice, whereby constraints, beliefs, and preferences (as total rankings) determine choices, they have not shown that this model is in fact successful in explaining or predicting behavior. Moreover, as Chapter 9 will document, the standard theory of choice has some serious empirical failings. Yet economists can do some things well, such as predicting the effects on revenue or trade balances of changes in tax rates. I doubt that there is any useful global judgment to be made. Presumably the standard model will work less well for agents who find themselves in unfamiliar contexts than in circumstances where individuals have had a chance to form reasonably stable and well-articulated preferences (although in such contexts, models that rely on habit rather than preferences might work just as well).

I return to these issues in Part III of this book, but first it is time to examine the connections between preferences and welfare.

PART II

PREFERENCES, WELFARE, AND NORMATIVE ECONOMICS

Welfare economists take welfare to be the satisfaction of preferences. Yet it is obvious that people sometimes make bad choices. (I certainly have.) People often prefer what is bad for them. It requires no philosophical acumen to recognize human fallibility. An uncharitable observer might conclude that economists are dunces. When defenders of cost-benefit analysis maintain that the "net benefit" of policies ought to influence public choices, they assume that what they call "net benefit" indicates preferences and that preferences indicate welfare. It seems there is a problem. Does welfare economics rest on a philosophical blunder?

Chapter 7 argues that preference satisfaction does not constitute welfare. Chapter 8 then turns around and argues that, with some crucial qualifications, economists are justified in taking preference satisfaction to measure welfare.

7

Preference Satisfaction and Welfare

This chapter argues that the satisfaction of preferences – even when preferences are informed, rational, and generally spruced up – does not constitute well-being. Economists are mistaken when they make claims such as "Policy x is deemed better than policy y for an individual if and only if, given the opportunity, the individual would choose x over y" (Gul and Pesendorfer 2008, p. 24). In assessing preference-satisfaction theories of well-being, it is crucial to understand correctly what is meant by "preference." For example, *if* preference were defined as a ranking in terms of expected benefit, then it would be true by definition that what individuals prefer would coincide with what they believed was good for them. *If* people's expectations were correct, preference satisfaction would coincide with welfare. And *if* people choose what they prefer, then, as Gul and Pesendorfer maintain, they always choose what is best for them.

In the investigation of preference-satisfaction theories of welfare, I shall interpret preferences as economists do – that is, as total subjective comparative evaluations. There is no plausible alternative. The everyday sense of preferences as overall comparative evaluations is unsatisfactory for the purposes of a theory that identifies welfare and preference satisfaction, because it implies that when moral commitments conflict with preference, adhering to moral commitment always makes individuals worse off. Although doing what is right may not always be good for people, it should not always be bad for people whose preferences lead elsewhere. If one wants to define welfare in terms of preference, then one should take preferences to be total comparative evaluations.

Moral philosophers often link welfare to the satisfaction of *desire* rather than to the satisfaction of *preference*. But it is more sensible to define welfare in terms of preference satisfaction. To say that welfare is preference satisfaction implies that Jack is better off with x than he is with y if and only if he prefers x to y, whereas to say that welfare is the satisfaction of desire apparently implies that x improves Jack's well-being if and only if Jack desires x, regardless of how he ranks x and anything else. But how could satisfying his desire for x make Jack better off unless Jack prefers having or doing x to not having or doing x? The view of welfare I am concerned with maintains that people are better off with x rather than y because in their total evaluation of x compared to y, people rank x more highly. Philosophers who have defended the view that the satisfaction of preferences constitutes well-being have typically required that preferences satisfy further conditions – for example that they not be influenced by false beliefs. I will discuss such qualified or modified preference-satisfaction views in Sections 7.3 and 7.4.

Section 7.1 presents the main theories of welfare that compete with a preference-satisfaction view, briefly notes their inadequacies, and explains why a preference-satisfaction theory of welfare appeals to economists. Section 7.2 summarizes well-known objections to preference-satisfaction theories of welfare. Section 7.3 presents a more plausible but ultimately unsuccessful defense of the identification of welfare and preferences, which rests on the claims that welfare is the satisfaction of properly "spruced-up" preferences and that actual preferences are proxies for spruced-up preferences. Section 7.4 argues that this defense fails and that welfare is not the satisfaction of preferences, no matter how one tweaks them.

7.1. WELFARE AND PREFERENCES

In speaking of people's welfare or well-being (which I treat as synonymous), I am talking about how good people's lives are *for them*, about how well their lives are going. Exactly what is good for a particular agent, Jill, will depend on Jill's character, ability, tastes, and circumstances, and what is good for Jill may be very different from what is good for Jack. Most of the differences between those things that make Jill's life go well and what contributes to Jack's well-being involve *instrumental* goods – things that are good for people because they are *means* to something else. If one focuses on *intrinsic* goods – things that are good for individuals without regard to their consequences – there is less variation across individuals. Bifocals may be good for Jill and bad for Jack, even though clear vision is good for both. Instrumental goods, such as bifocals, are good only if the ends to which they conduce are good. If nothing were good for people without regard to its consequences, then nothing at all would be good. There must be noninstrumental (that is, intrinsic) goods in order for there to be instrumental goods. A central problem of moral philosophy has been to determine what things are intrinsically good for human beings. Aristotle, for example, held that happiness, which he took to be a kind of flourishing, is the sole intrinsic good.

In everyday conversation, as in moral philosophy, one finds many views of what makes life go well. For example, although most people agree that loyal friends, robust health, and a buoyant sense of humor make one better off, whereas disgrace and failure in one's projects make one worse off, there are also many disagreements. Philosophers have attempted to systematize views of well-being by proposing general theories. These theories fall into three broad categories. First, there is the view that only mental states are intrinsically good. Exactly which mental states are intrinsically good is controversial. The best-known mental state theory is hedonism, the view that well-being consists in pleasure or happiness. Jeremy Bentham (1789) and, more controversially, John Stuart Mill (1861) are the best-known proponents. Henry Sidgwick defends the view that welfare is any mental state that is in itself desirable (1901).

Few contemporary philosophers defend mental state views. If Jill mistakenly believes that she is loved by her family and friends and that her projects have been successful, while Jack correctly believes just the same things, then their mental states may be the same. But it seems that Jack is better off (Griffin 1986, pp. 9–10; Nozick 1974, pp. 42–25; Parfit 1984, p. 494). Despite this compelling objection, some philosophers such as Feldman (2004) and Crisp (2006) still defend mental state views, as do a number of prominent contemporary psychologists and economists (Dolan and Kahneman 2008; Frey 2010; Frey and Stutzer 2001; Kahneman 1999, 2000a, 2000b; Kahneman and Krueger 2006; Kahneman and Thaler 2006; Layard 2006).

Most philosophers, however, have rejected mental state theories and have opted instead for either objective-list or preference-satisfaction theories. Objective-list theories maintain that a number of different things contribute to well-being. Some of these are mental states, but objective states of affairs such as success in worthwhile endeavors, friendships, and development of one's capacities also contribute to well-being (Griffin 1986, 1996). Objective-list theories are problematic, because the lists for different individuals may not coincide, and it seems that some further theory is needed to explain why items appear on Jill's and Jack's lists of intrinsic goods and why their lists differ.

One response to these difficulties for objective-list theories is to invoke an individual's preferences to explain what contributes to the individual's well-being and to shift to a preference-satisfaction view of well-being. But preference-satisfaction theories are problematic, too, because people often prefer what is worse for them over what is better, if only because of false beliefs. Although welfare and preference satisfaction thus do not coincide, many contemporary philosophers are wedded to the view that well-being consists in the satisfaction of self-interested "informed," "rational," or "laundered" preferences (Arneson 1990; Gauthier 1986, ch. 2; Goodin 1986; and possibly Griffin 1986).

As this very brief discussion shows, the theory of well-being is an unsettled area of philosophy. All the contending theories face serious difficulties. Given that mainstream economists invoke preferences to explain and predict choices, it is natural that they would look to levels of preference satisfaction as the basis for welfare judgments. If individuals are exclusively self-interested, then they will prefer x to y if and only if they believe that x is better for them than y is. If they are perfectly well-informed, then their beliefs will be true, and x is in fact better for them than y if and only if they prefer x to y. Accustomed as they are to the idealizing assumptions that individuals are self-interested and perfectly well-informed, economists are inclined to take well-being to be the satisfaction of preferences.

Economists have also defended their identification of well-being with preference satisfaction on the grounds of epistemic and philosophical modesty. Rather than attempting to say what is good for people, economists let people speak for themselves via their preferences. In Chapter 8, I maintain that this argument expresses an important truth, but it will take some work to find that truth. There is nothing philosophically modest about the claim that preference satisfaction determines well-being.

A third factor that has motivated economists to identify well-being with preference satisfaction is the aversion economists commonly feel toward paternalistic policies – policies like seat belt laws that coerce people for their own good. If whatever people prefer is best for them, then successful paternalism is not only ill-advised; it is impossible. But successful paternalism is not impossible. One can sometimes benefit people by coercing them. For example, suppose Jack is about to step into an open manhole, and the only way Jill can protect him is physically to push him aside. In doing so, she is successfully coercing him for his own benefit. Whether paternalistic policies are sometimes justified is a genuine question. Serious arguments against paternalism, such as John Stuart Mill's, give reasons why it is generally better not to coerce people for their own benefit, rather than asserting – absurdly – that people always choose what is best for themselves.[1]

Finally, economists who believe that welfare is a desirable mental state such as happiness might argue that the best way to promote happiness is to satisfy people's preferences. Even though the fact that Jack prefers x to y does not tend in any way to *make* x better for him, it could be that the best way to make Jack happy is to satisfy his preferences. Possible equivocations both on "utility" and on "satisfaction" make this view particularly tempting. "Utility" has been used to refer to pleasure as well as to indicate preference. So it is easy to think of what has more utility, in the sense of better satisfying preferences, as having more utility in the sense of providing more pleasure. "Satisfaction" can refer to a feeling as well as to whether the world matches the agent's preferences. These are not the same. If an agent does not know that a preference is satisfied, the satisfaction of that preference has no tendency to make the agent feel satisfied. The only connection between the satisfaction of a preference and a person's feeling of satisfaction seems to be that people typically feel more satisfied when they know that they have gotten what they want. Helped

---

[1] Mill's argument against paternalism appears mainly in chapter 4 of *On Liberty* (1859). The manhole example derives from Mill's example in chapter 5 of preventing someone from crossing an unsafe bridge. See also Dworkin (1971).

by these equivocations,[2] many economists may be "closet hedonists." Those economists and psychologists who have recently espoused hedonism, whom I mentioned earlier, do not make this bad argument. They recognize and indeed emphasize that people are bad at estimating future pleasures or remembering past pleasures. In their view, rather than relying on preferences, psychologists and economists should measure welfare by measuring people's moods.

7.2. WHY WELFARE IS NOT PREFERENCE SATISFACTION

False beliefs are not the only problem for preference-satisfaction views of well-being. A second difficulty (already discussed in Chapter 2) is that people care about other things in addition to their own well-being. People are sometimes altruistic and sometimes malevolent. People may sacrifice their own well-being to benefit or harm others. Satisfying preferences sometimes has no bearing on one's own welfare. Derek Parfit gives the following example:

Suppose that I meet a stranger who has what is believed to be a fatal disease. My sympathy is aroused, and I strongly want this stranger to be cured. We never meet again. Later, unknown to me, this stranger is cured. On the Unrestricted Desire Fulfillment Theory, this event is good for me, and makes my life go better. This is not plausible. We should reject this theory. (1984, p. 494)

What Parfit calls "the unrestricted desire fulfillment theory" says that, other things being equal, satisfying any of Jack's desires makes Jack better off. Parfit's criticism applies equally to a preference-satisfaction theory. If the stranger recovers, Parfit's preference that he recover rather than die is satisfied. But this does not make Parfit better off.

Preference changes constitute a third set of difficulties for the view that welfare is preference satisfaction (Bykvist 2010, Gibbard 1986, McKerlie 2007). Does one increase Jill's welfare just as much by changing her preferences so that she now wants what she gets as by changing the world so that she gets what she wants? Should the consequences for welfare of a policy that changes people's preferences be measured by people's preferences before the policy is put into place or by their preferences afterward? Should one care about satisfying preferences that a person no longer has, such as my son's childhood desire to drive a gravel truck (Brandt 1979, ch. 13; Parfit 1984, ch. 8)? At this point in his life, he thinks not. Why not? There are two plausible answers, but both assume that welfare is not preference satisfaction. First, he now knows more about himself and about the attractions of various careers than he did when he was three. So his current preferences

---

[2] Economists have no monopoly on equivocations on the word "satisfaction." For example, Wellman writes, "The outcome of an action can satisfy or fail to satisfy the actor's desires, that is, achieve or fail to achieve his goals. If the actor desires something and his actions achieve it ... then satisfaction results. Satisfaction, generically, encompasses such emotional reactions as happiness, pleasure, contentment, and relief" (1990, p. 106).

are more likely to track what will really make his life better. This answer supposes, however, that his preferences among careers depend on his *judgment* concerning what will make his life better in some other way than satisfying his preferences. Second, giving people what they no longer want is not likely to make them happy. But this answer supposes that well-being is happiness, not preference satisfaction.

Fourth, what should one say about welfare when there are inconsistencies in an agent's preferences or when there are conflicts between an agent's "first-order" preferences, such as a preference for smoking and "second-order" or "metapreferences" such as a preference that one not prefer to smoke (Frankfurt 1971, Sen 1977)? The axioms of ordinal utility theory rule out inconsistencies, but people do not always conform to the axioms. Tensions between first- and second-order preference can give rise to internal struggle, feelings of regret and deprivation, and apparently inconsistent behavior, such as purchasing cigarettes but then locking them away or flushing them down a toilet – and then running out to purchase more (Schelling 2006). If Jack prefers x to y, yet prefers possessing some other preference ranking to this one, is he better off with x than y?

Fifth, if one combines the view that welfare is preference satisfaction with views that take social policy to be concerned with promoting welfare, one is led to implausible policy recommendations in cases of expensive tastes and antisocial preferences. Suppose that Jack has cultivated a taste for fine wine and consequently is worse off than Jill, who has a similar income but is happy with beer. Should Jack get more resources because he needs more to satisfy his preferences (Arneson 1990, Arrow 1973, Dworkin 1981)? Or suppose that Jack is a racist or a sadist. Should the negative effects of satisfying his preferences be weighed against the "benefits" of satisfying them, or should one refuse to count the satisfaction of antisocial preferences as contributing to welfare (Harsanyi 1977, p. 56)?

It is also implausible to identify welfare with preference satisfaction when people's preferences are the result of previous coercion or manipulation or of problematic psychological mechanisms. Sometimes people want things precisely because they cannot have them ("the grass is always greener on the other side of the fence"), or they spurn what they think is beyond their reach, like the fox who judged the unobtainable grapes to be sour (Elster 1983; Sen 1987b). Preferences often depend heavily on factors that ought to be irrelevant, such as how choices are framed (which is discussed in Chapter 9). Those who are systematically denied roles in public life or equal shares of consumption goods may learn not to want these things. Such seems to be the condition of many of the world's women. As a result of systematic oppression, they may not have strong preferences for individual liberties, the same wages that men earn, or even protection from domestic violence. But liberties, high wages, and protection from domestic violence may make them better off than giving them what they prefer. When the preferences of oppressed people derive from their oppression, one cannot measure their welfare by considering how well their preferences are satisfied.[3]

7.3 WELFARE AND LAUNDERED PREFERENCES: THE APPROXIMATION RATIONALE

As we have seen, satisfying someone's preferences need not contribute to their welfare, because, among other reasons, their preferences might not be self-interested or because they may be based on false beliefs. Yet many distinguished contemporary moral philosophers believe that welfare and preference are closely linked:

> Versions of the desire theory now define the orthodox view of the nature of welfare, at least in the Anglo-American philosophical world. In the theory of rational choice the equation of well-being with utility (preference-satisfaction) has achieved the status of an unquestioned axiom, while in ethics its more prominent recent defenders have included Brian Barry, John Rawls, R. M. Hare, James Griffin, and Joseph Raz. (Sumner 1996, p. 122)

Probably the most common view of welfare is that it consists in the satisfaction of suitably purified preferences. For example, Peter Railton proposes that "an individual's good consists in what he would want himself to want, or to pursue, were he to contemplate his present situation from a standpoint fully and vividly informed about himself and his circumstances, and entirely free from cognitive error or lapses of instrumental rationality" (1986, p. 16). If well-being is the satisfaction of self-directed informed preferences and actual preferences approximate self-directed informed preferences, then it may be reasonable to measure welfare by the satisfaction of actual preferences.

It is more plausible to maintain that well-being is the satisfaction of purified preferences than to maintain that it is the satisfaction of actual preferences. On such a view, satisfying preferences that are not self-directed or that are based on ignorance or cognitive defects would not count as benefiting a

---

[3] Heathwood (2005) responds to objections based on false beliefs or distorted or manipulated preferences by pointing out that when desires are "defective," and their satisfaction is consequently bad for someone, it is typically the case that satisfying them frustrates some other and more important desire. Heathwood might be making a point that satisfying a desire may frustrate a preference for something the agent more strongly desires. Avoiding such confusions is a crucial advantage of formulating a theory of welfare in terms of preference satisfaction rather than desire satisfaction. Let us accordingly suppose that Heathwood means to defend a preference satisfaction theory. He is pointing out that when Jill quenches her thirst by drinking water that is, unbeknownst to her, polluted and that thus makes her sick, she in fact fails to choose what she prefers. In terms of her complete, transitive, and context-independent preference ranking, she prefers (*ex post*) not drinking the water to drinking it. Whatever the merits of this partial defense of an actual preference satisfaction view of well-being, it provides no comfort to welfare economists who take the satisfaction of her *ex ante* mistaken preferences as increasing rather than decreasing her expected well-being.

person. When actual preferences change, there need be no puzzle about how to make the person better off if the person's purified preferences have not changed. Conflicts among actual preferences are no problem if there would be no conflicts among informed preferences. One might also maintain (although this is more controversial), that racist, sadistic, or other antisocial preferences cannot withstand full information and rational scrutiny, and so those who are concerned to benefit people can discount such preferences.

7.4. WHY THE APPROXIMATION VIEW FAILS

The view that welfare consists of the satisfaction of properly purified preferences resolves many of the difficulties facing the actual-preference satisfaction view. It has the drawback that it makes an individual's level of well-being less easily measurable than does the actual-preference satisfaction view. If welfare is the satisfaction of informed and self-interested preferences rather than actual preferences, then in addition to determining people's preferences, welfare economists need to determine to what extent actual preferences coincide with informed self-interested preferences. It might nevertheless be reasonable in many cases to take actual preferences as a proxy for purified preferences.

The real problem with the approximation view is that its underlying account of welfare as the satisfaction of purified preferences is indefensible. The fact that Jack prefers x to y does not make it the case that x is better for him than y, no matter what conditions one imposes on his preferences. Consider the requirement that preferences be self-directed, which is introduced so as to avoid the implausible implication that satisfying Parfit's preference that the stranger be cured makes Parfit better off. What Parfit calls the "Success Theory" of welfare (in contrast to what he calls the "Unrestricted Desire Fulfillment Theory") takes well-being to be the satisfaction of preferences "about our own lives." But which preferences are about one's own life? Parfit maintains that if, unbeknownst to Jill, her child becomes a petty thief, that is bad for her because it frustrates her desire to be a good parent, and that desire is about her own life (1984, p. 495). On the other hand, Parfit argues that Jack's desire to have healthy children is not about Jack's own life. If, unbeknownst to Jack, his child dies, that death does not make Jack worse off (1984, p. 494). Clearly it is not going to be easy to say which preferences are "about" oneself and which are not. Mark Overvold (1984) proposes that self-regarding preferences are preferences concerning states of affairs that entail the agent's existence (see also Sobel 1998, pp. 266–69 and Griffin 1986, pp. 23–24).

But the distinction that is needed is not between those of Jack's preferences that are about himself and those that are about something else. If Jack prefers to harm himself, then his preference is certainly about himself, but satisfying it will not make him better off. The distinction that is needed lies between those of Jack's preferences that are directed toward promoting his own well-being and those that are not. That distinction presupposes some notion of well-being that does not derive from preferences (Sumner 1996, p. 135).

The fact that Jill prefers x to y does not make x better for her. Suppose Jill prefers alternative x to y and that this preference is as self-directed, rational, and well-informed as anyone could demand. Why should one conclude that Jill would be better off in the state of affairs where x obtains than she would be in the state of affairs where y obtains? One answer is that Jill finds out whether x or y obtains and is both pleased with x (her anticipation of her enjoyment may have been the reason why she preferred x to y) and pleased that her preference is satisfied. In that case, however, what makes her better off is not the satisfaction of her preference, but the pleasures she experiences because x obtains. Recall that for a preference to be satisfied is for the world to be as the agent prefers. Whether or not the satisfaction of a preference contributes to the agent's *feeling satisfied* is a separate question (Kraut 2007, pp. 98–99).

Suppose that when Jill finds out that her preferred state of affairs x obtains, x's obtaining has no positive effect on Jill's mental state. Are there still any grounds to conclude that the fact that x obtains implies that (*ceteris paribus*) Jill is better off? How does Jill's preference ranking by itself make the fact that x obtains good for Jill? Richard Kraut puts the challenge in the following way:

More precisely: is it the case that whenever S wants (rationally, with proper information, and reflectively) P to occur, and P does occur, that is good for S simply *because* it is something he wants in that way?

[This view implies that when] our desires just happen to reach out to objects that are not in themselves worth wanting, and when they motivate us to acquire those objects [and we succeed in doing so], that is good for us. (2007, p. 118)

Consider again Parfit's example of his preference that the stranger be cured. This seems to be a case where satisfying a preference does not increase well-being. Should one conclude, as Parfit and others have, that his is the wrong sort of preference, or should one conclude instead that satisfying preferences does not by itself contribute to well-being? The fact that Parfit's preference that the stranger be cured intuitively has nothing to do with him is, I suggest, irrelevant. For example, suppose that Jill prefers it to be the case that she be descended from Charlemagne or that Jack forms a preference that he be a chimera.[4] Jill's and Jack's preferences are about themselves. Suppose

---

[4] More specifically a "tetragametic chimera," a human being whose body is made up of two genetically distinct lines of cells derived from a total of four gametes – eggs and sperm. Such chimeras exist. In one instance, doctors in Boston hoping to find a donor for a woman who needed a kidney transplant discovered that only one of her three sons had a genome that could be a descendent of the genome they found in their mother's blood. The mother's contribution to the boy's DNA traced back to the DNA in one of the two fertilized eggs that fused and became this woman, whereas the blood cells from which her DNA was taken derived from the other egg. There may be a tangible advantage to being a chimera, because one's body is then compatible with more prospective organ donors. But this possible advantage does not depend on Jack's preferring to be a chimera.

further that these are not idle wishes. Both go to considerable trouble to find out whether their preferences are satisfied. Suppose that although their preferences are in fact satisfied, Jill cannot trace her ancestry, while the genetic tests Jack undergoes miss the organs whose DNA would show that he is a chimera. So neither knows that their preferences are satisfied. Is there any reason to believe that the satisfaction of Jill's and Jack's self-regarding preferences makes their lives in any way better? The fact that a state of affairs satisfies people's preferences does not make the state of affairs good for them. Preference-satisfaction theories of well-being are mistaken.

Another way to support this conclusion is to ask what moral "pull" satisfying someone's preferences should have on others. In my view, like Thomas Nagel's (1986, ch. 9), none at all. If something is valuable to people *only* because they want it, then their getting it has *no* direct moral importance for others. I have reason to help others to get what they want only if I can see how what they want is worth wanting, or why their lives will be in some way better if they get what they want. For example many Boston residents desperately wanted the Red Sox to win the World Series in 2004. Their happiness when the Red Sox won gave others – even Yankees fans – some reason to judge it to be good for them that their preferences were satisfied. But, as Nagel maintains, the mere preferences of Red Sox fans, as opposed to their happiness or unhappiness, is of no moral importance to others. Because the welfare of others, unlike the satisfaction of their preferences, is of moral importance, welfare cannot be the satisfaction of preferences.

Views that take welfare to be the satisfaction of self-interested and rational preferences seem more acceptable than theories that take welfare to be the satisfaction of actual preferences, in part because they provide a foot in the door for arguments concerning objective goods, goods that ought to be preferred (Railton 1986; Griffin 1986, p. 30). To take well-being to be the satisfaction of purified rather than actual preferences shifts the emphasis from what people do prefer to what they should prefer:

> The shift to informed desires also represents an important change in the role of desires as determinants of well-being. If a full appreciation of the ways in which my life would be changed if I could speak French well would lead me to have a strong desire to master that language, then it is likely both that I have reason to do this, and that doing it would contribute to my well-being. But what role does the desire that I would have play in making these things true?" (Scanlon 1998, p. 115)

For example, if what were truly intrinsically good consisted of happiness, then one could argue that it is rational for those concerned with their own welfare to prefer happiness to unhappiness. But the purified preference for happiness over unhappiness would not explain why happiness is better.

How could defenders of preference-satisfaction views have gone so wrong? The answer lies in failing to distinguish a preference-satisfaction theory of well-being, which maintains that satisfying a preference makes someone better off, from claims that satisfying preferences contributes to well-being conceived of in some other way. Satisfying preferences does usually contribute to well-being, because individuals know when their preferences are satisfied or frustrated, and getting what one wants makes one feel pleased. Or if one prefers x to y because one enjoys x more, then satisfying one's preference will increase one's enjoyment and contribute to one's welfare for that reason. In addition, as James Griffin (1986), Joseph Raz (1984, ch. 12), and Thomas Scanlon (1998, pp. 118–21) point out, achieving a worthwhile objective to which one has devoted oneself makes people better off. So whether the achievement of some worthwhile objective contributes to Jill's well-being depends on whether Jill has devoted herself to it. And whether she has devoted herself to it in turn depends on her preferences. For example, although the survival of Siberian tigers contributes relatively little to most people's well-being, if Jill dedicates herself to protecting them, and her activities are successful, that success makes her life go better. So Jill's choice of projects, which depends on her preferences, matters to whether a state of the world makes her life better off. It is because of Jill's preferences that the worthwhile objective of saving Siberian tigers became one of her projects and that the success of this objective enhances her life. Although Jill's preferences play a crucial role in determining whether some outcome makes her better off, her well-being rests on the success of her worthwhile projects, not on the satisfaction of her preferences (Raz 1984, p. 291n).

7.5. CONCLUSIONS

It is easy to conflate the satisfaction of a preference with enjoyment or with the success of a worthwhile project or with a feeling of satisfaction at knowing that things are as one preferred. So it is tempting to link well-being to the satisfaction of preferences – at least once one purges preferences of the effects of false beliefs and narrows preferences to those concerned with oneself. Because economists see individuals as mainly self-interested and preferences as reflecting all evaluative considerations relevant to choice, they are tempted to identify preference satisfaction and welfare. But as this chapter has argued, welfare is not preference satisfaction, no matter how spruced up the preferences may be. What then remains of welfare economics?

8

Preferences in Welfare Economics

Chapter 7 showed that satisfying preferences does not by itself contribute to welfare. Preference satisfaction theories of welfare are untenable. This conclusion puts normative economists in an awkward position because it seems that their work rests on an untenable theory of welfare.

This chapter argues that welfare economics does not rely on a mistaken theory of welfare. It argues that welfare economics presupposes no *theory* of welfare at all. Rather than constituting well-being, preference satisfaction can serve as evidence of well-being, regardless of what theory of welfare one accepts. In defending this apparently paradoxical thesis, this chapter offers guidelines concerning when the tools of standard normative economics can be used justifiably to address specific problems.

Section 8.1 argues that preferences sometimes provide useful evidence concerning what is good for people. If (1) individuals seek to benefit themselves and (2) are good judges of what is good for them, then they will prefer what is better for them to what is worse. Their preferences will correspond to what is good for them, because their preferences depend on their judgments of what is good for them, rather than because their preferences make things good for them. Section 8.2 explores some implications of this view for practical work in normative economics and especially for cost-benefit analysis. Section 8.3 comments briefly on recent work on preference distortions and paternalism, and Section 8.4 offers conclusions.

8.1. PREFERENCES AND WELFARE: AN EVIDENTIAL VIEW

Chapter 7 argued that Jack's preferring x to y does not make it the case that x is better for him than y, no matter how purified his preferences may be. But Jack may prefer x to y because he believes that x is better for him, and his beliefs may be correct. So his preferences may tell others what is good for him. This third-person evidential connection between preference satisfaction and well-being justifies some applications of welfare economics (Scanlon 1998,

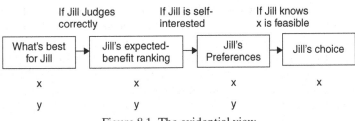

Figure 8.1. The evidential view.

pp. 116–18). When people are self-interested, their preferences will match what they believe will benefit them. If with respect to the matters at hand individuals are good judges of what will benefit them, then economists can use people's preferences as evidence concerning what promotes their welfare. This reasoning is illustrated in Figure 8.1. Suppose there are only two alternatives, x and y, and that x *is* in fact better for Jill than y. *If* Jill judges correctly, then Jill will rank the expected benefit of x above that of y. *If* Jill is self-interested, then Jill prefers x to y. If Jill knows that she can choose x or y, she will then choose x.

The economist can then work backward. From Jill's choice, the economist can infer Jill's preference – but only on the assumption that Jill knows that she could have chosen y. From Jill's preference for x over y, the economist can infer that Jill thinks that x is better for her than y is – but only on the assumption that Jill is self-interested. From Jill's judgment that x is better for her than y is, the economist can conclude that x is in fact better for her – but only on the assumption that Jill's judgment is correct. In this way welfare economists can draw inferences concerning well-being from people's choices without committing themselves to any theory of well-being. Although what people prefer does not *determine* what is good for them, it is sometimes *evidence* concerning what is good for them. As Elliott Sober pointed out to me, just as Socrates in Plato's *Euthyphro* said of piety that it is loved by the gods because it is holy rather than holy because loved by the gods, so I contend that an alternative is preferred by self-interested and well-informed people because it is good for them, not good for them because they prefer it.

Even in contexts where people are not completely self-interested and in which their beliefs are flawed, their preferences may be the best guide a third party has to what is beneficial to them. Legislators and bureaucrats usually know less of the circumstances of an individual such as Jill than she knows, and they generally have a less wholehearted concern for her well-being than Jill does. The judgments of legislators about how to make Jill better off are likely to be worse than her own judgments. It is also *safer* to rely on people's preferences than on the judgment of government officials. The mistakes individuals make about their own good can, to some extent, cancel out, and bureaucrats or legislators will not arrogate to themselves the power to substitute their judgment for people's own judgments. Treating individuals as authoritative judges of their own interests is also one way of showing respect for them. These considerations do not justify blanket deference to people's preferences. In some contexts, self-interest does not predominate. In others, people's beliefs are badly mistaken or their preferences are systematically distorted by factors such as framing. Of course, even then people might wind up preferring what is better for themselves, but only by dumb luck. When people are bad judges or are not seeking their own advantage, there is little reason to take their preferences to be evidence concerning what will benefit them.

These considerations constitute grounds for diffidence about overruling preferences and they identify sketchily the factors that determine whether it is reasonable to take preferences as indicating welfare. At the same time they undermine the assumption that, regardless of the circumstances, there is reason to satisfy people's preferences. Recall that *the fact that some alternative satisfies someone's preference does not make that alternative better for that person.* It is easy to forget this by sliding between thinking of utility as merely an indicator of preference and thinking of utility as pleasure or welfare. For example, if one describes Jack's charitable preferences by stating that Haitian earthquake relief is an argument in Jack's utility function, then it seems to follow that giving relief to the victims of the earthquake "gives utility" to Jack – that is, makes Jack better off. But it only follows in virtue of an equivocation on the meaning of "utility." Preferring x to y implies judging that x is better than y, *all things considered*, not judging that x is better *for oneself* than y. To avoid equivocating, this book sticks to the official meaning of utility as an index of preference and, when commenting on the relations between preference, self-interest, and welfare, avoids using the word "utility" altogether.

People can distinguish between the questions, "Which is better, all things considered?" and "Which is better for me?" Having distinguished the two questions, it could be the case that the only considerations someone finds relevant are how x and y bear on his or her interests. Such complete self-interest would be unusual and very difficult to carry out, because it is often impossible to guess which alternative is best for oneself. What most people judge to be best and what they judge to be best for themselves will not always coincide, because most people think that other considerations than their own interests are relevant to their evaluations of alternatives.[1]

---

[1] It may also be the case that someone prefers x to y, even though they do not believe that x will be better for them, because they judge that being known to prefer x to y is advantageous. For example, in *Les Liaisons Dangereuses*, the Vicomte de Valmont pretends to be charitable to help seduce Madame de Tourvel. In this case, Valmont has no real preference for relieving the suffering of the poor – he just wants to appear to have such preferences. But agents may easily acquire a genuine preference for x over y because of the advantages of having that preference, not because they judge x to be better for themselves than y. One should distinguish the value to an agent of having a preference (and being known to have a preference) from the value to an agent of the alternatives the agent prefers.

When people prefer x to y, it is often the case that x is better for them than y. For this reason economists can often measure welfare by preference satisfaction. The reason for this correlation is that self-interest is common, and people are often better judges of what serves their interests than are others. There is no other stronger connection between preferences, welfare, and self-interest.

Consider, for example, attempts to measure the "non-use" or "passive-use" values of natural resources by means of contingent valuation, which in effect consists of asking people how much they are willing to pay to protect a marsh or an endangered species (Arrow et al. 1993). Although the assumption that people's preferences reflect their well-founded judgments of what will benefit them is reasonable in some contexts, following Sagoff (2004), I conjecture that willingness to pay to protect the environment is not mainly driven by people's expectations of how much they personally will benefit. For example, suppose that Jill is in her eighties and does not expect that climate change will diminish the quality of her life. What happens after her death will not make her happier or less happy. Yet she believes that people have an obligation to be good stewards of the earth, and she is consequently willing to pay a good deal (in the form of higher energy costs) to limit greenhouse gas emissions. If economists measure the effect on her welfare by determining how much she is willing to pay to limit greenhouse gas emissions, they will get the wrong answer, because her willingness to pay reflects her moral convictions, not her judgment of what will benefit her. Contingent valuation studies are usually misleading measures of the impact of the environment on people's welfare (Sobel 1998, p. 251). Willingness to pay for environmental protection greatly overstates the welfare consequences of environmental protection.[2] Unless there is some reason other than the promotion of welfare why policies should be sensitive to people's preferences, contingent valuation studies of non-use value should not influence policy.

In arguing that people's preferences for environmental preservation or protection of endangered species are not mainly self-interested, I mean that they do not derive mainly from people's judgment concerning how much species or ecosystems contribute to their own lives. What matters is not whether preferences *concern* the agent, but whether the preferences are directed toward the agent's own well-being. Recall the examples discussed in Chapter 7 of Jill's preference that she be a descendant of Charlemagne and Jack's preference that he be a chimera, which obviously concern themselves. If Jill does not believe that there is any advantage to her of being a descendant of Charlemagne, then, albeit self-directed, her preference is not self-interested.

---

[2] Policies that secure some environmental protection may bring to fruition some project of Jill's, and in that way they may contribute to Jill's well-being, but the measure of benefit to Jill is not her preferences.

If she is right that there is no advantage for her, then whether her preference is satisfied does not bear on her well-being.

The evidential view does not support any version of a preference satisfaction theory of well-being and has few implications for philosophical theories of welfare. It claims that, regardless of what philosophical theory of human well-being one accepts (other than an actual preference satisfaction view), preferences indicate well-being. If well-being turned out to be happiness, then the preferences of self-interested individuals without mistaken beliefs would tell economists what makes them happy. If well-being were some set of objective goods, the preferences of those who are self-interested and well-informed would tell economists which objective goods most promote welfare.

One might question whether economists can avoid committing themselves to any theory of well-being. An economist cannot regard people's preferences as evidence concerning what is good for them, unless he or she has some notion of what is good for people. Economists must rely on some idea of well-being to distinguish between self-interested and non-self-interested preferences and to decide when people are good judges of what serves their interests. It might thus appear that the evidential view of the relationship between preferences and welfare gives economists a way of jumping out of an uncomfortably warm preference satisfaction frying pan directly into the fierce philosophical fire that heats it.

To reach conclusions about whether people are good judges of what benefits them and to determine whether their preferences are self-interested, economists need to know something about what is good for people, but they do not need a philosophical *theory*. For example, environmental economists can easily see that the continued existence of Siberian tigers contributes to individual welfare because they know that enjoyment contributes to welfare and that people enjoy looking at Siberian tigers and imagining them in the wild. On the other hand, economists can see that for most people the existence of Siberian tigers does not bear significantly on components of the good life such as friendship, health, or successful accomplishment of worthwhile projects. This argument assumes, as people typically do, that pleasures, friendship, health, and accomplishment contribute to well-being. Common platitudes concerning what makes people better off, unlike a serious objective list theory of well-being, offer no exhaustive list of intrinsic goods and depend on no philosophical theory that specifies what things are intrinsically good for people and why. Yet platitudes concerning what is good for people still have content. Economists and everyday folk do not have to wait for a satisfactory philosophical theory of welfare before they can say anything about what makes people's lives better or worse. Welfare economists, like the rest of us, have many beliefs about what makes people better off, although their philosophical modesty makes them reticent about trumpeting those beliefs. Their beliefs are likely to be imperfect. Economists may be prone to exaggerate the importance of material possessions in a good life. Be that as it may, economists know enough about the things that make lives good or bad that they can make sense of the evidential view of the relationship between preference satisfaction and welfare.

8.2. THE EVIDENTIAL VIEW AND THE SCOPE OF COST-BENEFIT ANALYSIS

As a practical matter, welfare economics influences policy evaluation mainly via cost-benefit analysis, and the rest of this chapter will focus on cost-benefit analysis, but similar claims can be made about any method of evaluating policies in terms of welfare, where welfare is measured by the extent to which preferences are satisfied. In theory, welfare economists aspire to specify a social welfare function – a function that evaluates social states on the basis of the preferences of the individuals affected by those states. There is little agreement concerning the exact form of such a social welfare function, and in practice, formal economic appraisals of policies or investments almost always take the form of cost-benefit or cost-effectiveness analysis.[3]

Cost-benefit analysis assesses policies in terms of their "net benefits": the total amount the beneficiaries of a policy would be willing to pay to implement the policy minus the total amount that those who would prefer that the policy not be adopted would require in compensation for agreeing to the policy.[4] These amounts are typically imputed from observations of market transactions, although sometimes people are simply asked. Suppose, for example, that in some economy, 1 million bushels of wheat are produced annually by peasants who employ horse-drawn plows. As sharecroppers, they split the output with landlords. Tractors are then introduced, and agriculture is transformed. Demand for the labor of peasants and the use of their horses drops, as does the peasants' share of the increased output of 1.1 million bushels, which is reduced to 200,000 bushels. If we assume that utility (as a representation of preference) is a linear function of the quantity of wheat, Figure 8.2 depicts the situation.

---

[3] Cost effectiveness analysis, which I shall not discuss, compares the costs of bringing about some specified benefit. So, for example, economists could compare the cost per life saved of laws requiring the use of seat belts to the cost per life saved of laws requiring that manufactures install air bags. Cost effectiveness analysis, unlike cost-benefit analysis, does not permit economists to compare policies designed to bring about different benefits.

[4] Net benefits can be calculated instead summing what economists call "equivalent variations" rather than, as described in the text, by summing "compensating variations." In terms of equivalent variations, the net benefit is the sum of the total amount that beneficiaries of a policy would need to be paid to be as well off as they would be if the policy had been instituted minus the total amount that those harmed by the policy would pay to keep the policy from being instituted. The differences between these two ways of measuring net benefits are not relevant to the argument of this chapter. For general presentations of cost-benefit analysis, see Boardman et al. 2010, Broadway and Bruce 1984, Layard and Glaister 1994, Pearce 1983, and Sugden and Williams 1978.

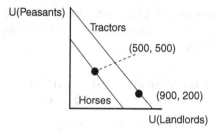

Figure 8.2. Net benefit.

The inner line represents distributions of wheat and preference satisfaction that the horse technology makes possible. The outer line represents possible distributions of the greater output of the tractor technology. The actual change from the initial distribution of half a million bushels to both peasants and landlords to the new distribution of 900,000 bushels to the landlords and 200,000 bushels to the peasants is not necessarily a social improvement. For example, if one were to make interpersonal comparisons of the extent to which preferences are satisfied, the average level of preference satisfaction might be much lower. Or one might condemn the situation as unjust regardless of any judgment of overall welfare.

Cost-benefit analysis makes no interpersonal comparisons of preference satisfaction, and it is agnostic concerning distributional justice. Cost-benefit analysts instead distinguish between questions of "efficiency" and questions of equity. Cost-benefit analysis determines which policies provide the greatest "net benefit," where net benefit is defined by the difference between what the "winners" from the new technology (the landlords in this case), should be willing to pay to introduce the new technology (400,000 bushels), and the amount that the losers (the peasants) will demand to compensate them for agreeing to the tractor technology (300,000 bushels). The policy with the greatest net benefit has the greatest capacity to satisfy preferences (Kaldor 1939; see also Hicks 1939).[5] If willingness to pay indicates preference satisfaction, then the

---

[5] This last conclusion is, in fact, unjustified. Consider the following possibility:

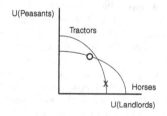

The two curves represent the extent to which the preferences of peasants and landlords can be satisfied by the use of the horse or tractor technology. Point X is a potential Pareto improvement over point O. By redistributing the output from landlords to peasants (a movement

policy with the greatest net benefit apparently has the greatest *capacity* to satisfy individual preferences. And if preferences are evidence of welfare, the policy with the greatest net benefit apparently has the greatest capacity to make people better off.

The policy with the greatest net benefit may nevertheless be ethically undesirable because of distributional considerations, with respect to which the cost-benefit analyst claims no expertise. Welfare economics is concerned only with efficiency with respect to the promotion of welfare (Le Grand 1991) or the satisfaction of self-interested preferences. The job of welfare economists is to advise policy makers on how to expand the "pie." The ethical question of how to distribute the pie can be left to others to address.

Cost-benefit analysis raises many questions beside those concerning the relations between preferences and welfare, which are the concern of this chapter. For example, willingness to pay depends on wealth as well as preferences. So cost-benefit analysis gives more weight to the preferences of someone who is rich than to the preferences of someone who is poor. In theory, this problem can be solved. Assumptions concerning the character of the social welfare function provide principled ways of adjusting willingness-to-pay information to cancel out the unjustified influence of differences in wealth or income (Fankhauser et al. 1997). But practical applications rarely make these adjustments. Furthermore, the techniques employed to measure net benefits – whether from surveys or from market behavior – raise further difficulties. These difficulties with cost-benefit analysis are not relevant to the discussion here, and for the purposes of the argument, let us suppose (contrary to fact) that net benefit measures increased capacity to satisfy preferences.

Net benefit will be a relevant consideration in welfarist policy evaluation if (1) economists are able to measure it, (2) net benefit measures capacity to satisfy preferences, (3) preferences concerning policies and their consequences are mainly self-interested and undistorted, and (4) people's expectations concerning the consequences of policies for their own well-being are not worse than other projections. Retrospectively, what matters is whether people's expectations are correct, and when they are mistaken and bad policies are put in place, it is not much of a consolation to know that there was no better basis for policy. What matters *ex ante* are how well supported people's expectations

---

along the tractor curve), one can achieve an actual Pareto improvement. But O is also a potential Pareto improvement over X. By redistributing the output from the horse-based agriculture from peasants to landlords, one can again achieve an actual Pareto improvement. Given that the economic "pie" cannot get larger both if one shifts from using horses to tractors and if one shifts from using tractors to horses, potential Pareto improvements cannot logically imply a greater capacity to satisfy preferences or to increase welfare. If one utility possibility curve lies completely within another, as in Figure 8.2, then there is an increased capacity to satisfy preferences. See Scitovsky 1941, Samuelson 1950, and Broadway and Bruce 1984, pp. 99–101.

are. For the purposes of argument, this chapter grants conditions (1) and (2) and focuses on conditions (3) and (4).

More specifically, what this chapter proposes is that before applying cost-benefit analysis, economists concerned with promoting welfare should ask whether people are likely to be good judges of their own interests with respect to the effects of the policy alternatives under consideration and whether people's preferences concerning effects of the policies are motivated by self-interest. These are not simple questions, and their answers are bound to be controversial. But mindless application of cost-benefit analysis or blanket condemnation of it is controversial, too. Asking whether it is reasonable to assume that preferences are accurate and self-interested helps economists judge when welfare economics can sensibly guide policy. Understanding that preferences are evidence of well-being helps those who aim to promote well-being judge when to take willingness-to-pay information as a basis for policy evaluation.

Some economists believe that cost-benefit analysis should help policy makers satisfy well-informed preferences, regardless of whether preferences are self-interested, rather than to help policy makers promote welfare. For example, Vining and Weimer take cost-benefit analysis to provide "a framework for comprehensively taking account of the full range of social benefits and costs" (2010, p. 1; see also Zerbe et al. 2006). They assume not only that policies should be sensitive to distributional considerations (an assumption with which most practitioners of cost-benefit analysis would agree), but that measures *of the net benefit* of policies should depend in part on the extent to which those policies satisfy distributional preferences.

An alternative approach to measuring the social benefits of improvements to the circumstances of the least advantaged is based on the observation that many people derive utility from helping the disadvantaged. In other words, they are willing to pay something to help the most disadvantaged. The spontaneous outpouring of charitable giving after major disasters is one indication of such altruism. (Vining and Weimer 2010, p. 22)

To "derive utility from helping the disadvantaged" could mean "are made better off by helping the disadvantaged" or "prefer to help the disadvantaged." Willingness to pay to help the disadvantaged reveals people's preferences, but it does not tell economists whether satisfying them makes helpers better off. If helpers are altruists, then they are not seeking their own advantage, and there is no reason to believe that satisfying their preferences benefits them. If what Jack cares about is Jill's welfare, satisfying Jack's preferences makes Jill rather than Jack better off and may lead to double-counting of her welfare. But Vining and Weimer are not welfarists. Rather than taking net benefit to be a measure of the capacities of policies to promote welfare (of "efficiency") that combine with distributional considerations ("equity") to determine policy, Vining and Weimer would make net benefit a measure of social value that takes into account efficiency in the promotion of welfare as well as citizen's views of equity in its distribution.

Although respect for popular sovereignty demands that the ethical views of a population ultimately govern, there is much less reason to defer to the population's distributional preferences than to their self-interested preferences. If legislators take for granted that people are decent judges of what is good for them, then the objective of increasing welfare gives legislators reason to institute policies that satisfy self-interested preferences. The objective of increasing welfare gives them no reason to institute policies that satisfy preferences that are not self-interested. The legislator must instead ask whether there are good reasons supporting non-self-interested preferences, and if he or she thinks there are not, then the legislator should attempt to change the minds of his or her constituents. Citizen's willingness to pay for distributive justice (or for environmental amenities, historical preservation, protection of endangered species, or climate control) may not accurately express their true preferences concerning the values of these things. Preferences are comparative evaluations, not the heavings of guts, and without having the feedback that comes with ordinary consumption or the opportunity for thoughtful reflection on specific distributional questions, few people will be able to determine what their preferences are. When asked about their willingness to pay, they will answer, but those answers will not reflect settled valuations. In part for this reason, representative governments place a number of road blocks (in the form of legislative procedures, a bill of rights, and minority protections) in the way of responding to the ethical views of citizens.

Whether or not distributional decisions should be governed by willingness to pay, the proposal to incorporate distributional and other non-self-interested preferences into cost-benefit analysis requires a different justification for the practice than the one provided in this chapter. Although some distributional preferences may be self-interested, there is no reason to maintain that satisfying distributional preferences generally promotes welfare. It is not obvious that policy should always aim to increase welfare, because policies that improve the welfare of the malicious, envious, or malevolent may be objectionable regardless of their consequences for the welfare of others. This chapter will not tackle this question, however. Instead it takes for granted the popular view that concerns about welfare should largely govern policy and focuses on the question of when preferences can be taken as a guide to welfare.

Welfare economists may not welcome the inquiries they need to make to determine whether preferences are good evidence of welfare, but concerns about whether preferences are self-interested and well-informed already influence the decisions economists make about how to gather information on willingness to pay. As Adler and Posner point out, cost-benefit analysts already avoid measuring non-self-interested preferences:

The USDA does not ask animal rights activists whether they care about the existence of slaughterhouses. The U.S. Postal Service does not ask individuals whether they care about the existence of pornography in the mail. Funding agencies do not ask people how much they would be willing to pay to prevent those agencies from funding morally controversial research projects involving stem cells. (2006, pp. 126–27)

In each of the cases Adler and Posner mention, there is an element of self-interest. For example, animal rights activists would be happier if there were no slaughterhouses. But their preferences are not mainly self-interested, and taking them into account would be a way of making animals rather than people better off. Although many benefits would accrue to people from ceasing to slaughter animals for food and hides, the animal rights activists' willingness to pay for eliminating animal slaughter does not measure these benefits.

Once one recognizes that the point of welfare economics in general or cost-benefit analysis in particular is not satisfying preferences per se, but using people's preferences as evidence to guide in the promotion of welfare, additional possibilities open up. If willingness to pay to protect the environment does not reflect people's expectations of the extent to which they will benefit from environmental preservation, one can ask people how much they expect to benefit rather than what they are willing to pay. It is the expectation of benefit that matters. For example, rather than asking people, "How much would you be willing to pay to prevent whooping cranes from going extinct?" economists can ask them, "Give a monetary estimate of how much worse your life would be if whooping cranes went extinct. What drop in income would be equivalent in its effect on your welfare to the extinction of whooping cranes?" I conjecture that the monetary estimate of benefit would be much less than the willingness to pay. If people's willingness to pay for preventing whooping cranes from going extinct expresses their judgment of how much the existence of whooping cranes contributes to their lives, the answer to the second questions should instead be at least as large as the answer to the first. So in addition to eliciting the information that is truly relevant, surveys of this sort would serve as an empirical test of my claim that willingness to pay for environmental protection greatly overstates the welfare benefits to the current generation.

Implementing this proposal sensibly, like implementing a contingent valuation measurement, would be a complicated task. Figuring out how to estimate the welfare consequences to future generations would be an additional problem. But once economists recognize that the relationship between preferences and welfare is evidential rather than constitutive, there is no longer any reason why welfare economists should limit their inquiries to preferences. When preferences are not self-interested and there are other ways to learn about people's expectations of benefit, economists should explore those other ways.

With respect to environmental protection and global warming, putting cost-benefit analysis on a conceptually coherent basis could have political consequences that I personally would regret. A conceptually coherent measure of the welfare benefits of these policies (for currently existing adults) would, I conjecture, show them to be far lower than current contingent valuation methods imply. Yet I personally favor stricter environmental protections and severe limitations on emissions of greenhouse gases. If I thought that policies should aim exclusively to promote the welfare of this cohort, then I would need to change many of my views about environmental protection. But I do not think that environmental policy should aim exclusively to promote welfare, let alone the welfare of only this cohort and so would not be shaken by a demonstration that environmental protection makes a far smaller contribution to current welfare than contingent valuation studies imply. But not everyone sees the issues this way, and in this instance, conceptual clarity could be harmful politically.

Recognizing that the connection between preferences and welfare is evidential also implies that net benefit calculations should depend only on undistorted preferences that reflect accurate or well-justified beliefs. The issues here play a prominent role in the controversy over so-called *ex ante* versus *ex post* approaches to cost-benefit analysis (Broome 1991b, ch. 7; Hammond 1983; Harris and Olewiler 1979; Hausman and McPherson 1994). The *ex ante* approach takes the expected level of preference satisfaction, which depends on the subjective probabilities of the individuals in question, to measure welfare. The *ex post* welfare approach takes the extent to which preferences are in fact satisfied by the outcome as the measure of welfare. The *ex ante* approach evaluates outcomes in terms of *ex ante* preference satisfaction, whereas the *ex post* approach (which must, of course, also assess alternatives prospectively if it is to guide policy choice) evaluates outcomes in terms of "objective" expectations of preference satisfaction – that is, expectations that rely on objective probabilities.

Although the *ex ante* approach, which asks no questions about whether individuals have mistaken beliefs, has many defenders, it is difficult to defend policy choices that rely on preferences based on misapprehensions (Hausman and McPherson 1994). Adler and Posner provide some nice examples of the way this realization already influences practice:

> Before asking them about air quality over the Grand Canyon, the EPA showed survey respondents photographs of the site with different levels of pollution. The EPA's goal was presumably to provide information on environmental aesthetics, about which respondent's intrinsic preferences were uninformed. For a regulation involving labeling of meat and poultry products, the USDA relied on CVs [compensating variations] for health benefits people would enjoy if they altered their behavior in response to the labels, rather than people's CVs for nutrition disclosure. The agency appeared to take the intrinsic preference (for health) as a given and to circumvent the problem of imperfectly informed instrumental preference (for nutritional disclosure).[6]

---

[6] Adler and Posner 2006, pp. 127–28. The information concerning the EPA is from Deck 1997, p. 267, and the information concerning the USDA is from Department of Agriculture 1991. "CVs" are "compensating variations" mentioned in footnote 4 to this chapter.

As these examples show, economists can take steps to provide people with better information, to correct mistaken beliefs, and to avoid relying on distorted preferences, including preferences based on false beliefs. Contemporary psychology has identified contexts in which people are likely to make mistakes, and policy analysts can use these findings to help decide whether to take people's preferences as guides to their welfare. One advantage of understanding that preferences are total comparative evaluations is that economists and regulators can make clear sense of people's preferences being *mistaken*. What connects preferences and welfare are people's judgments about what serves their interests.

Accepting the view that the connection between preferences and well-being is evidential rather than constitutive permits economists to avoid offering any philosophical theory of well-being. It also spares those who believe that policy should depend in part on interpersonal comparisons of welfare the hopeless task of explaining how to make interpersonal comparisons of preference satisfaction. Interpersonal comparisons of well-being will not be easy on any view of well-being, but the conceptual difficulties of comparing the "extent" to which Jill and Jack's preferences are satisfied are particularly daunting (Hausman 1995). This interpretation of the relation between preference and welfare makes clear that whether net benefit should guide policy depends on whether willingness-to-pay information provides good evidence concerning what individuals believe to be beneficial to themselves and whether individuals are good judges of what is beneficial to themselves.

8.3. PREFERENCE DISTORTIONS AND PATERNALISM

In asking, "Is this a context in which individuals are good judges of what is beneficial to themselves?" one is really asking two questions: "Is this a context in which individuals are well-informed? and "Is this a context in which the preferences of individuals are undistorted?" Recent investigations that reveal systematic flaws in decision making (which is discussed in Chapter 9) help answer the last question. The cost-benefit analyst should avoid relying on net benefits when preferences are distorted by decision-making flaws because the flaws provide a good reason to doubt that preferences are a good guide to the individual's welfare. Examples of such flaws include overconfidence, exaggerated optimism, status quo bias, inertia, inattention, myopia, conformity, akrasia (weakness of will), and addiction. When economists observe that a much higher percentage of employees enroll in retirement plans when that is the default (and they need to check a box to opt out) than the percentage who enroll when the default is not to enroll, they have reason to doubt that enrollment choices are grounded in an accurate judgment of which alternative is better for the employee. The factors responsible for the disparity – status quo bias, inertia, and inattention – distort preferences.

When preferences are distorted, one cannot rely on them to indicate what makes people better off. But is that the end of the story? Is there nothing more that welfare economists can say? Instead of quitting, or relying on preferences, regardless of how distorted they may be, some prominent economists and political theorists have proposed a set of policies that they call paternalistic (Camerer, Issacharoff, Loewenstein, O'Donoghue, and Rabin 2003; Thaler and Sunstein 2003a, 2003b, 2008;). If policy makers can determine what is truly good for individuals, then they can devise policies that will lead people to make better choices. The most prominent defenders of this view, Richard Thaler and Cass Sunstein, argue that one can nudge people's choices without limiting their freedom. Whether this is so is not relevant to the discussion here (but see Hausman and Welch 2010). What is relevant is the need for some grounds, independent of the distorted preferences agents express, to determine what is good for the agents.

For example, by determining the default, government policy or the owner of the firm can "nudge" individuals to save more or less for retirement. But to know which nudge to give, one needs to know which would be better for individual employees. How are economists or policy makers supposed to know this? Thaler and Sunstein place considerable weight on the agent's own retrospective judgment (or *ex post* preferences). They write, "a policy is "paternalistic" if it tries to influence choices in a way that will make choosers better off, *as judged by themselves*" (2008, p. 5). But retrospective judgments are exposed to many of the same distorting factors. (Are the regrets of those who are about to retire at how little they saved any more reliable as a guide to their welfare than the repentance of an aged libertine as a guide to his?) Any set of policies that aims to direct people's choices for their own good relies on substantive judgments concerning what is good for people.

Platitudes may help. Economists do not need to elicit preferences to know that policies that lower infant mortality, that lessen workplace injuries, or that provide safe drinking water are, other things being equal, good for people. In the case of retirement savings, platitudes tell us that it is good to save and that individuals are often myopic. But at the same time we know that out of exaggerated caution, people may save too much and pass up opportunities to live well. And when considering policies that lower infant mortality, lessen workplace injuries, or provide safe drinking water, other things are rarely equal. There are almost always costs, which need to be measured and compared to the benefits. There are few good alternatives to relying on preferences or individual judgments of expected benefit.

Another possibility, which is implicit in some of Thaler and Sunstein's proposals, is to attempt merely to counteract the effects of distortions, without taking the further step of pushing individuals to make one choice rather than another. So, for example, one might make it a condition of employment that an applicant pass a test concerning the terms of the firm's retirement plan and choose whether or not to enroll. Such a requirement counteracts the distortions and forces the employee to be informed without pushing individuals either to enroll or not to enroll. Rather than setting a uniform retirement savings policy, it forces individuals to choose for themselves.

Many policy choices do not permit such an option. Whether to preserve some habitat, unlike how much to save for retirement, is not something that each individual can choose for himself or herself. The best economists can do when they recognize the flaws in people's deliberative capacities is to minimize their influence. For example, economists assessing the benefits and costs of a new power plant should recognize that willingness to pay to reduce the probability of a power failure in the next decade will be affected by people's myopia and their inability to adjust for probabilities. On the other hand, people's willingness to pay to prevent the food in their refrigerator from spoiling today or to avoid being without light or air-conditioning this evening should be relatively undistorted. Willingness to pay to avoid spoiled food or a sweaty night in the dark provides better evidence concerning some of the benefits of the power plant than willingness to pay to avoid power failures during the next decade. As the examples from Adler and Posner indicate, those who are thoughtful and proficient at the craft of cost-benefit analysis are already aware of homely generalizations such as this one. Rather than telling them something surprising, the discussion places these generalizations in a broader context: To guide policies well, economists need to measure well-informed and undistorted expectations of benefit or harm. Preference measurement is a means to this end.

8.4. CONCLUSIONS

This chapter argues that when preferences are self-interested, well-informed, and undistorted, they are a good guide to what benefits people. When these conditions are met, it is sensible for those seeking to promote welfare to employ methods of appraising policies such as cost-benefit analysis that rely on information concerning preference satisfaction. When these conditions are not met, it makes sense to take steps to purify people's preferences of mistake and distortion so as to widen the domain in which these conditions are met and to attempt to measure expected benefit rather than preferences. The complexities are daunting.

There are many other problems. Consider, for example, the Congressional Budget Office's cost-benefit analyses of increases in the gasoline tax and of increases in the average fuel economy demanded of new cars (Dinan and Austin 2004). These analyses use market data that show how much people are willing to pay for larger and more powerful vehicles in order to impute costs from driving smaller, lighter, and less powerful cars. Presumably, the preferences implicit in car purchases are largely self-interested, and car buyers are reasonably well-informed about the alternatives they face. No doubt there are some distortions due to inertia, and advertisers attempt to play on longings for status and sex appeal that car ownership might magically produce. But it seems that preferences among cars are just the sort that cost-benefit analysis should rely on. Yet even in such a "clean" case, there are further complications. Because the advantages of a larger and faster car depend in part on the size and speed of other cars, reducing the size and acceleration of all cars could be almost as costless as getting people at sports events to avoid standing up to see better. If regulations or taxes make all cars smaller, someone who now needs a Hummer to be the king of the road could have much the same experience in an SUV weighing half as much (Frank 2000). Car purchases plausibly reflect people's judgments of which cars will be best for them, given the distribution of other cars on the road. These preferences are not necessarily relevant when what is in question are policies that will change that distribution. When the benefits or costs are in this way relational, they do not add up. In the case of relational goods, something that, acquired by one person, increases his or her welfare, may have no benefit when acquired by lots of people.

The point of this example is that cost-benefit analysis is not a mechanical method of determining which policy is most capable of promoting welfare. The finding that policy P has a greater net benefit than policy Q does not always show that it has a greater capacity to satisfy preferences, and even if it had a greater capacity to satisfy preferences, those preferences may not be good evidence of what will make people better off, because the preferences may not be self-interested or because they may be distorted or depend on false beliefs. Yet we have no other quantitative guide to policy making, and policy makers need the information that cost-benefit analysis aims to provide. As D. W. Pearce describes the situation:

> Those who practised CBA had a real-world task to attend to. Someone had to decide on the priorities within any sub-budget of government expenditure. The niceties of academic interchange in the learned journals did little to aid those who had these tasks. Instead, it seemed that not only did CBA offer a technique for aiding the evaluative process, albeit subject to many caveats, it actually offered the *only* reasoned technique. (1983, p. 21)

This is a serious point, but to provide helpful information, those who do cost-benefit analysis must employ it cautiously and with good judgment. Bad advice is not always better than no advice.

PART III

PSYCHOLOGY, RATIONAL EVALUATION, AND PREFERENCE FORMATION

Part III of this book is concerned with empirical investigations of people's preferences and of how people construct and modify those preferences, as well as with normative questions about how people ought to construct and modify their preferences. Chapter 9 discusses empirical investigations of choice and preference carried out by psychologists and behavioral economists, which make clear how unsatisfactory it is in general to suppose that preferences are just "given" and not subject to rational evaluation. It also draws a contrast between the standard model of choice economists employ and the way psychologists theorize about action. Examining the role of context in the construction of preference leads naturally to the issues Chapter 10 explores concerning theories of preference formation and modification. Chapter 11 concludes this book.

9

The Psychology of Choice

This chapter discusses empirical evidence concerning how people evaluate alternatives and make choices and how this evidence bears on the standard model of choice and the axioms governing preference to which economist are committed. It also compares the standard model of choice to ways in which psychologists theorize about action. These are large topics, but the issues I shall address are relatively narrow.

At the core of choice theory are the axioms discussed in Chapter 2: completeness, transitivity, context-independence, and choice determination. If people were able to carry out total comparative evaluations of all the alternatives they face, one would expect these axioms to be true. But economists do not believe that people's preferences are always complete, transitive, and context-independent. The axioms are approximations or idealizations. The fact that people violate transitivity when presented with enough pairwise choices does not imply that economists should not model the typical consumer's weekly grocery shopping as governed by a transitive total subjective ranking. Even the demonstration that some plausible methods of evaluating alternatives lead to intransitivities (e.g., Tversky 1969) need not be alarming if those methods are unlikely to be important in the domain in which economists apply the standard model of choice.

In addition to unsystematic divergences of actual behavior from the axioms of ordinal utility theory, which are neither surprising nor particularly disturbing, cognitive psychologists such as Daniel Kahneman, Sarah Lichtenstein, Paul Slovic, and Amos Tversky, and a new generation of behavioral economists influenced by them, have demonstrated experimentally that people's choices differ *systematically* from the predictions of choice theory. This literature casts doubt on the explanatory and predictive merits of choice theory both because of the discrepancies it documents and because of the regularities it formulates and corroborates, which conflict with the implications of standard choice theory. The alternative theories psychologists and behavioral economists have proposed have drawbacks, but these are not always so serious as to justify

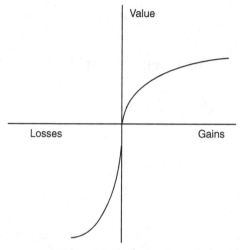

Figure 9.1. Loss aversion.

dismissing them. Among the many relevant phenomena that psychologists and behavioral economists have identified, this chapter considers the implications of two classes of results: (1) loss aversion, framing, and the endowment effect; and (2) reversals, variance, and adaptation of preferences.

9.1. LOSS AVERSION, FRAMING, AND THE ENDOWMENT EFFECT

Many experiments show that individuals anchor their evaluation of alternatives to a reference state of affairs, typically the status quo. Given that reference, people weigh losses more heavily than gains with both marginal losses and marginal gains of diminishing importance. People's choices reflect a value function shaped like this (Figure 9.1).

Like a standard preference ranking, this value function is supposed to determine choices, but unlike a preference ranking, it depends on the reference point and so is definitely not context-independent. The asymmetry between gains and loses is a central element in prospect theory (Kahneman and Tversky 1979). Loss aversion is manifest in the so-called endowment effect (Kahneman, Knetsch, and Thaler 1991) whereby individuals demand more to part with some commodity than they would have been willing to pay to acquire it.

Because the reference point so heavily influences the value of alternatives, it is possible to get people to make contradictory evaluations of the same alternatives by means of descriptions that shift people's reference points. So, for example, consider the following two responses to a disease that affects 600 people:

Program A	saves 200 people
Program B	saves 600 people with probability 1/3
	saves no one with probability 2/3

When asked which they prefer, about three-quarters of experimental subjects prefer program A. Other experimental subjects were asked to compare Programs C and D:

Program C	400 people die
Program D	no one dies with probability 1/3
	600 people die with probability 2/3

Faced with a choice between C and D, about three-quarters of experimental subjects prefer program D (Tversky and Kahneman 1981). Yet A and C are descriptions of exactly the same state of affairs, as are B and D. The same outcomes look different depending on whether subjects take as the reference point the death of 600 people (and one's action as saving 200 for sure or 600 with a probability of one-third) or whether subjects take the reference point as all 600 living.

Because people weigh gains and losses differently, their choices depend on the reference point. Rather than unsystematic failures of the axioms, these data identify an additional systematic influence on choice. As Kahneman, Knetsch, and Thaler put it:

> It is in the nature of economic anomalies that they violate standard theory. The next question is what to do about it. In many cases there is no obvious way to amend the theory to fit the facts, either because too little is known, or because the changes would greatly increase the complexity of the theory and reduce its predictive yield. The anomalies that we have described ... may be an exceptional case, where the needed amendments in the theory are both obvious and tractable. The amendments are not trivial: *the important notion of a stable preference order must be abandoned in favor of a preference order that depends on the current reference level.* A revised version of preference theory would assign a special role to the status quo, giving up some standard assumptions of stability, symmetry and reversibility which the data have shown to be false. But the task is manageable. (1991, p. 205 [italics added])

The crucial points are first, that these anomalies show that the influence of the diverse factors that motivate people cannot be summarized in a single ranking that is complete, transitive, context-independent, and choice determining; and second, that some of the divergences are systematic and predictable. Preferences depend significantly and regularly on the reference point from which individuals evaluate alternatives.

9.2. REVERSALS, VARIANCE, AND ADAPTATION

A second set of anomalies shows that people's rankings of relevant considerations may be constructed on the fly in the course of decision making. This finding is plausible: When one thinks about the enormity of the task of evaluating everything relevant to any specific choice, it makes sense to economize on mental effort and fill in one's preference ranking only as needed. This possibility does not imply that economists are mistaken to simplify and to treat preferences as if they were fully articulated before deliberation begins. But as the experimental evidence shows, the processes that generate rankings in the course of decision making do not regularly result in preferences that satisfy all the axioms. The rankings implicit in choice behavior often depend on factors that are irrelevant to a total subjective evaluation of relevant considerations. This dependence undermines the explanatory and predictive claims of the standard model of choice.

There is a great deal of evidence revealing how slippery, changeable, and distorted preferences can be. Some of this has been known for millennia and embodied in popular sayings. In the case of phenomena such as sour grapes (see Elster 1983), a change in constraints leads to a change in preferences, in violation of context-independence. Experimental results over the past two generations reveal more striking problems. In the experiments showing the existence of *preference reversals* (Lichtenstein and Slovic 1971), individuals are given a choice between two gambles of roughly equal expected monetary value. For example, one gamble pays off \$4 if a roulette wheel comes up with any number other than 36 and has a loss of \$1 if the ball lands in slot 36. A second gamble pays off \$16 if the ball lands in slots 1–11 and loses \$1.50 if the ball lands in slots 12–36. The expected monetary values of these gambles are \$3.85 and \$3.86, respectively. Some people prefer the safer bet; others prefer the bet with the larger payoff. No surprises so far. What is remarkable is that among those who choose the safer bet, nearly three-quarters are willing to pay *more* for the bet with the larger payoff. Their expressed preference is the opposite of the preference implicit in their willingness to pay.

Preference reversals were predicted by Slovic and Lichtenstein (1968) before they ran the experiments that displayed the phenomenon, and the findings have been replicated many times, including in a Las Vegas casino, where individuals were gambling their own money (Lichtenstein and Slovic 1973). Economists who have attempted to make the phenomenon go away by better experimental design have failed (Grether and Plott 1979; but see Chu and Chu 1990). How preferences are elicited affects how experimental subjects think about the alternatives and construct their preferences. Tversky and Thaler draw the following conclusions:

The discussion of the meaning of preference and the status of value may be illuminated by the well-known exchange among three baseball umpires. "I call them as I see them," said the first. "I call them as they are," claimed the second. The third disagreed.

"They ain't nothing till I call them." Analogously, we can describe three different views regarding the nature of values. First, values exist – like body temperature – and people perceive them and report them as best they can, possibly with bias (I call them as I see them). Second, people know their values and preferences directly – as they know the multiplication table (I call them as they are). Third, values or preferences are commonly constructed in the process of elicitation (they ain't nothing till I call them). The research reviewed in this article is most compatible with the third view of preferences as a constructive, context-dependent process. (1990, p. 210)

Rather than carrying around bulky mental tablets in which alternatives are etched in order of their total subjective evaluation, individuals carry around notes on the advantages and disadvantages of different alternatives, their properties, and their consequences. Faced with the need to make a decision, agents compile these notes and construct a fragment of a ranking. Shortcuts are unavoidable, and they result in predictable flaws. As preference reversals show, how preferences are elicited can influence what people prefer. The preferences people construct depend on what people are asked to do and how the problem is framed (Slovic and Lichtenstein 2006b, p. 2).

The implications of this picture of individuals evaluating alternatives "on the fly" go deeper. For example, in a recent paper, Simon, Krawczyk, and Holyoak report on experiments that show:

[A]s people processed the decision task, their preferences for the attributes of the alternative that was ultimately chosen increased, while their preferences for the attributes of the to-be-rejected choice decreased.... In general, both the reported values of the attributes (ratings of desirability) and their weights (ratings of importance) shifted to make one alternative dominate the other.... These findings cannot be attributed to differences in methods used to elicit or describe the options, nor to variations in context (cf. Slovic, 1995; Tversky & Kahneman, 1986). Rather, the reconstruction of preferences seems to be the natural outcome of the very process of decision making. (2004, p. 335)

The experiments Simon, Krawczyk and Holyoak are discussing ask subjects to compare jobs that differ across four dimensions – office space, commuting time, salary, and vacation time – and they show that to bolster and rationalize their choices, subjects adjust both the importance they attach to these dimensions and their assessment of how good or bad the chosen alternative is with respect to these dimensions. Rather than choosing on the basis of a preexisting total subjective ranking that, in accord with a hedonic pricing model, implies a consistent valuation of the attributes of the alternatives, the subjects adjust their preferences to rationalize their choice, which in turn results mainly from an evaluation in terms of a single dimension that the experimental subject finds particularly salient.

The connections between preferences and choices reflect the influence of deliberation on evaluation at the same time that they reflect the influence of evaluation on choice. Evaluating attributes, states of the world, and alternative actions is a deliberative process analogous to deciding. The standard model of choice posits fully articulated comparative evaluations that do not exist. To suppose that all the factors that motivate people can be summarized in a single total subjective ranking is often not an innocent simplification. The evaluative attitudes that drive choice are typically too fluid and shifting, and the rankings they imply are heavily dependent on a contextually determined reference point. Rather than given, relatively fixed traits of individuals that (together with beliefs and constraints) drive choice, preferences depend on the context and the process of deliberation.

9.3. BELIEF-DESIRE PSYCHOLOGY

Compared to economists, psychologists have been more concerned with what specifically motivates people, and with how people deliberate and choose when facing specific kinds of problems, than with the general structure of deliberation and choice. Apart from work that borders on economics (such as Tversky and Kahneman's prospect theory), one finds in psychological treatments of choice examinations of motivating factors, inquiries into the ways in which desires arise and demand attention, studies of heuristics that govern deliberation, and explorations of how children acquire concepts of belief and desire. Similarly, research in marketing on the factors influencing consumer behavior is concerned with the nitty-gritty factors that make commodities and brands attractive. Among the determinants of preferences discussed by textbooks such as *Consumer Behavior: Buying, Having, and Being* (Solomon 2004) are needs (both utilitarian and for fun), underlying values, conceptions of the self, lifestyle, status, culture and subcultures, norms, advertising, and point-of-purchase stimuli. In place of an austere theory of choice determined by constraints, beliefs, and final preferences, with some discussion of how those final preferences arise from factors influencing the evaluation of alternatives, psychologists study individual motivating factors and the ways in which they combine in specific contexts to influence choices.

To illustrate the difference, Figure 9.2 juxtaposes the standard model of choice presented in Chapter 4 to Henry Wellman's well-known depiction of a simple version of belief-desire psychology, which I take to be typical of the views of many psychologists.[1] There are three points to emphasize about this comparison. First, preferences play no special role in psychologist's accounts of choice, and the word is often not mentioned at all. When preferences are mentioned, they are often treated as a species of desire. So, for example, Wellman writes:

By preferences I mean generalized dispositions toward certain things such as "preferring basketball over baseball" or generally "liking to ride horses." Preferences therefore are desire states somewhat akin to wants; compare, for example, "Liking

---

[1] The right-hand side of Figure 9.2 is borrowed from Wellman (1990), p. 100, figure 4.1, with the addition of an arrow between belief and desire in accordance with his figure 4.2, p. 109.

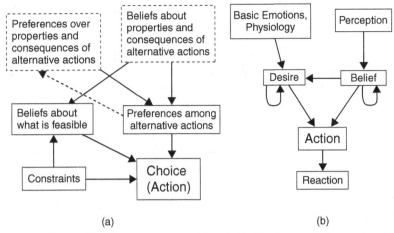

Figure 9.2. The standard model vs. belief-desire psychology.

to ride horses" and "wanting to ride that horse." Preferences figure prominently in explanations of recurrent activities. (1990, p. 103)

Wellman does not require that preferences be comparative. He has in mind by preferences something more like stable tastes than comparative evaluations (1990, p. 158).

Second, Wellman's model and the standard model are both elaborations of folk psychology – the view that people's choices are determined by their reasons, which are given by their beliefs and desires. The claims these two models make about the world are compatible. What they disagree about is how to sort the relevant factors and to structure explanations and predictions.

That leads to the third difference: the way the standard model and Wellman divide up the causal factors. The standard model supposes that all conflicts among desires have already been resolved in the individual's preferences among possible alternative actions. Apart from its derivation of final preferences, the standard model asks no questions about where preferences or beliefs come from or how reactions to the outcomes of actions may influence future beliefs, preferences, and choices. The relation between choice and its causes (beliefs, constraints, and preferences) is simple and determinate. Wellman's model, in contrast, calls for an account of how desires arise, especially from physiological states such as hunger and basic emotions such as fear, and it also calls for an account of how beliefs derive from, among other things, perceptions. At the other end, psychologists are concerned about the reactions that actions provoke and how those reactions change desires or beliefs. Wellman's model does not explicitly mention constraints, which play their role in defining the choice situation. Unlike the standard model with its strong conditions on preferences, there is no commitment to a stable motivational structure in terms of which choices can be explained.

Simple versions of the psychologist's model say little about how conflicts among desires are resolved. Psychologists have generally been less interested than economists in tying together a descriptive model of how people choose with a normative model concerning how they should choose rationally. Without any precise account concerning what should be done when desires conflict, Figure 9.2b is not an account of rational choice. The "desire" box in Figure 9.2b can contain anything that motivates people: moral commitments, whims, fundamental values, promptings of generosity or spite, aversions, appetites, conformity to social conventions, ambitions, passions, aspirations, and so forth. What makes these many things desires is their functional role rather than their phenomenological feel or their valence.[2] Desires are diverse, and more than one will usually be relevant to the agent's deliberations. These features of the psychologist's model make it flexible. Whatever generalizations experimenters may establish concerning factors influencing choices (other than beliefs and constraints) can be located in the "desire" box in Figure 9.2.

Because the psychologist's model of belief-desire psychology does not require that desires satisfy formal conditions like those imposed on preferences, the model avoids the empirical refutations to which standard choice theory has been subject. But it avoids these refutations at the cost of making few predictions. For this reason, its flexibility might be regarded as a deficiency rather than a virtue. In contrast to prospect theory, for example, which preserves choice determination even as it gives up context-independence and modifies completeness and transitivity, belief-desire psychology is more like a framework in which to locate specific theories of choice than itself a predictive or explanatory theory.

9.4. EXPLAINING AND PREDICTING PREFERENCES AND CHOICES

How should economists and decision theorists respond to the findings of psychological experimentation and the models of psychological theorists? We have seen that completeness and context-independence are both questionable approximations. People's rankings of alternatives depend heavily and consistently on features of context that distinguish gains from losses. Choices do not derive from beliefs and a single total subjective ranking. What factors do drive them? Without an answer – without some account of what determines preferences – economists have little to say.

The arguments presented in Part I and the experimental findings discussed in this chapter leave decision theorists and economists with a modeling choice.

---

[2] Schroeder offers a sophisticated view of desires (2007, pp. 156–57) along the same lines. His account is roughly as follows. Suppose Jack does *a*, when he believes some proposition *r*, which he finds salient and which explains why doing *a* promotes *P*. For Jack to desire that *P* is for him to be in a psychological state that grounds his disposition to do *a* when he believes *r*. In other words, desires explain why reasons lead to actions.

They can continue to require that preference determines choice and to treat factors such as loss aversion, endowment and framing effects, and rationalization as affecting preferences, or they can regard these factors as opening a gap between preferences and choices. For the same reasons that I rejected Sen's call for a multiplicity of preference concepts, I favor the first alternative: to treat preferences as determining choice and to regard the factors that influence choices investigated by psychologists as acting via their influence on preferences. This response to the experimental findings requires a retreat to a weaker context-dependent notion of preferences. In applications in which the context is fixed, this retreat has few costs. Even in applications where neither the context nor the preferences are fixed, if economists and decision theorists continue to regard preferences as determinative, then they can still employ consequentialist and game-theoretic models and the mathematical tools that permit predictions to be derived from them.

Because the data demonstrate that preferences depend on context, descriptive-choice theory can no longer take preferences as simply "given" – although there are contexts in which regarding crucial preferences as fixed before deliberation begins is a reasonable approximation. As a general rule, however, economists and decision theorists need to consider *how* preferences depend on context. They face the task of developing more substantive theories of preference formation than the thin consequentialist accounts to which they are already committed.

At this point, many economists would complain that the theories of preference formation that are needed will not draw on the techniques or models or explanatory generalizations that economists employ. However vital they may be, such theories are not within the scope of even an expanded economics. Investigating how physiological needs give rise to drives or how perceptions shape beliefs are not tasks for economists. If all theories of preference formation were like accounts of how physiological needs shape preferences, this complaint would be justified. But, as hedonic pricing models illustrate, there are things to be said about preference formation that draw heavily on the tools that economists already employ but have not yet become a standard part of mainstream economics. Although I do not defend the detailed claims that prospect theory makes, it illustrates another way in which economists could address questions of preference formation. Like the standard model, it takes values and "decision weights" to determine choices, but unlike the standard model, it takes both to depend on features of the context such as the reference point.

Although prospect theory may be gradually gaining ground (Wakker 2010), it has not been popular among economists, and the conclusions of this chapter may not win me many friends among economists either. Setting aside some problematic details, the main feature of prospect theory that puts economists off is that some of the behavior it describes is rationally indefensible and subjects agents to the possibility of exploitation. For example, someone who favors one course of action when its effects are described in terms of people saved, but who makes the opposite choice when the very same alternatives are described in terms of deaths, may be acting in accord with prospect theory. But, as people concede once alerted to what they are doing, such choice behavior is not rational. This fact does not refute prospect theory, because irrational behavior is clearly possible. But irrational behavior is often unstable, because people can learn, for example, to recognize framing effects and can adopt strategies to avoid making choices that are in this way irrational. In addition, if preferences do not satisfy the standard axioms, then it will be hard to justify the claim that satisfying people's preferences makes them better off, which – as discussed in Part II – is fundamental to welfare economics.

This chapter should be unsettling to orthodox mainstream economists. Experimental findings reveal serious problems for the standard model of choice, which suggest that economists and others who use the model need to attend more carefully to the factors that determine preferences. Whether this is a task for economists and how it is to be done – how evaluation should be understood – is the topic of the following chapter.

Constructing Preferences

Chapter 10 aims to reinforce two conclusions: that preferences, like judgments, are subject to rational scrutiny – that they are not just matters of taste – and that economists need to model preference formation. In doing this, it assembles elements out of which economists can construct models of preference formation. If preferences were complete and settled before economists go to work, it would not matter how preferences are formed. But if economists took preferences among the immediate objects of choice to be givens, they would have little to say about behavior, other than that people choose what they prefer. In addition, as we saw in the last chapter, people's preferences often depend on features of the choice situation, and economists need to understand how.

Preferences are the end of a complicated and largely untold story with a great deal of cognitive structure. It is hard to construct a total comparative evaluation. To do so, agents need to identify the alternatives and their properties and to weigh the considerations that count in favor of alternatives or against them. Agents must explore the causal pathways from actions to outcomes and determine the probabilities and the values of the consequences.[1]

Preferences are the outcomes of demanding and poorly understood processes of comparative evaluation. They cannot sensibly be regarded as mere feelings, to be determined by examining how one's gut heaves. Because it is difficult to ascertain one's preferences, people take shortcuts, and their

---

[1] An anecdote illustrates just how much is demanded to apply expected-utility theory. "Around 1956 Raiffa received an offer from Harvard Business School; he had a hard time deciding whether to stay at Columbia or go on to Harvard. Ernest Nagel in the philosophy department tells the following story. They happened to live in the same building on Claremont Avenue. One day Raiffa and Nagel came out of the apartment house at the same time, and Nagel said, 'Well, Howard, how are you coming with deciding between Columbia and Harvard? It shouldn't be difficult for you; you're an expert in decision theory!' Howard replied, 'Ernest, are you kidding? This is serious!'" Available at http://www.stat.columbia.edu/pdf-files/twatranscript.pdf, p. 9.

seat-of-the-pants evaluations often fail to generate preferences that satisfy the basic axioms or that accurately express the agent's considered evaluation. Economists rely on simplifications concerning the structure of preferences, the derivation of preferences, and the content of preferences. There are contexts in which it is legitimate to assume that agents have preferences that satisfy the basic axioms, but this assumption is often untrue. There are contexts in which it is legitimate to accept some consequentialist stories of preference formation, even though they are too simple. There are also contexts in which it is legitimate to rely on simple generalizations concerning the content of preferences, such as "People prefer more commodities to fewer." Yet preferences often do not satisfy the basic axioms, consequentialism often distorts preference formation, and people's preferences are not always acquisitive.

The real story concerning what people buy, how they invest, or what careers they choose is not one that any single discipline can tell. Many factors influence people's preferences. Some of these were canvassed in Chapters 4 and 9, but there are many others. If, as I shall continue to argue, the factors that affect choices should be treated as influences on preferences rather than as determinants of choice that compete with preferences, then models of preference formation remain to be articulated, and economists should play a large role in developing them.

10.1. HOW PEOPLE EVALUATE ALTERNATIVES

Chapter 4 and 9 mentioned four sources of preferences: (1) means-end reasoning, (2) attribute-based valuation, (3) emotional influence, and (4) physiological needs. The first two of these show how (guided by beliefs) desires or judgments of value transfer their "charge" to other desires and preferences. Means-end reasoning, as represented abstractly in expected-utility theory, derives preferences over alternative actions from preferences over their possible consequences and beliefs about the probabilities of those consequences. Multi-attribute utility and hedonic pricing models permit economists to infer attitudes toward attributes from choice behavior and to derive preferences among actions and their consequences from attitudes toward their attributes.

Psychological modeling of the effects of emotions and physiology has generally been less formal and narrower in scope. Recent work drawing on advances in neurology is, however, changing that (e.g., Glimcher et al. 2009; Litt et al. 2009). Although much of the work on preference formation that one finds in psychology or consumer research will not lend itself to the constrained maximization modeling that characterizes economics, the resemblances between decision making and preference formation suggest that economists have a good deal to contribute. For example, concerns about status and relative income drive many consumer choices, and Robert Frank (1987; Frank and Cook 1996) has shown how to adapt economic tools to model their impact. In addition, economists need to accommodate within their models the findings of psychologists concerning the flaws that deform decision making and the heuristics that guide and sometimes distort people's reasoning.

Consumer research, which is carried out in business schools rather than economics departments, documents other influences on consumer preferences, which economists cannot safely ignore. "Needs" – both utilitarian and for diversion – drive preferences (Solomon 2004) via manipulable consumer beliefs about how commodities and services satisfy those needs. For example, Holt (2005) tells the striking story of how Corona beer dramatically increased its market share by establishing a connection in consumer's minds between drinking Corona and relaxation on a peaceful beach: "What Corona's American consumers bought when the slapped down $7.00 for a six-pack of the former bargain basement beer was a chance to experience, through the ritual gulp of the yellow liquid, a glimmer of the American idea of a tranquil beach vacation" (Holt 2005, p. 283).

Drinking a Corona beer has many consequences individuals value. Many of these are consequences of drinking any beer, such as quenching thirst or intoxication. Others differ with the kind of beer. Although some of the British may disagree, I find lagers more refreshing than bitters or stouts (at least if the beer is cold and the day is hot). The experience of drinking a beer also has many characteristics that people value. It is an affordable opportunity to indulge oneself, just as one pleases. Accordingly, it is an opportunity for self-expression and self-definition. These simple generalizations permit one to formulate models whereby the value of drinking a specific brand of a specific kind of beer depends on the value the consumer attaches to what the consumer believes to be its attributes and consequences. Marketing and advertising can then influence demand by influencing the consumer's beliefs about those attributes and consequences. Whereas the Corona advertisements may have affected consumer choices in many ways, one of their effects was to change people's inchoate beliefs about how relaxing it was to drink this beer or what drinking a Corona meant. Modeling techniques that economists already employ can be adapted to study this way in which marketing influences demand.

Consumption preferences are complicated. As Belk (1988) argues, people often regard commodities as extensions of their bodies, and the extent to which individuals identify with things can have a vast influence on preferences. Major purchases mark milestones in people's lives. What kind of car they drive or where they live may define what kind of people they are. Consumption establishes relationships with commodities and brands (Fournier 1998) and with other consumers (Muniz and O'Guinn 2001), and these relationships in turn shape preferences. Consumer preferences are also governed by self-imposed rules (Amir et al. 2005), emotional reactions (Bagozzi et al. 2000), and cultural identifications (Solomon 2004). There appear to be many causal stories to be told. Even though economists have little to contribute to many of them, they can help tell some.

10.2. HOW PEOPLE OUGHT TO EVALUATE ALTERNATIVES

In addition to asking about what in fact influences preferences, those who study choices, preferences, and beliefs can ask normative questions: What ought (rationally) to influence preferences? How should individuals evaluate alternatives? In what ways can preferences be criticized? When are preferences rationally indefensible? When are they mistaken? Given that preferences or the values on which they depend constitute *reasons* for choices and hence justify as well as explain choices, questions about the rational defensibility of preferences are unavoidable.

None of the factors that affect preferences invariably do so in rationally defensible ways, and few, if any, seem always to exert an unjustified influence. Unless the values people attach to the consequences or attributes of alternatives are indefensible, consequentialist reasoning and attribute-based evaluation are rational ways of constructing and modifying preferences. Emotions and physiological needs can also play justifiable roles in preference formation. When Jack abruptly stops his hike and quietly backs down the trail after sighting a grizzly bear ahead munching on berries, his fear-driven preferences for a prompt exit are rational. Indeed his fear arguably encapsulates rapid instrumental reasoning (Lehrer 2009, p. 41). On the other hand, if Jack's fear leads him to cry out and run, it will not serve him well. Like emotional reactions, social or cultural norms may play a legitimate and justifiable role in the formation of people's preferences, or they may lead to mistaken or unjustified evaluations and actions.

Merely knowing what category of causal factor influences preferences does not enable one to justify or criticize preferences. One needs to know more about the details and especially about how agents adjudicate among the factors affecting preferences. How should the various influences on desires "add up" to determine and justify a total subjective evaluation?

10.3. AN EXAMPLE: HEALTH-STATE VALUES

Unlike desires, which often come unbidden and need not be compatible with an individual's other desires and values, preferences rest on a weighing of competing considerations and depend on judgments concerning the merits of the alternatives that are being compared. Sometimes the comparisons are trivial. Jill is thirsty. She sees a water fountain. She has good reason to drink and no reason not to drink. So she prefers drinking to not drinking.

One learns more about what goes into preference formation and when it is rationally defensible by examining harder cases such as the following: To assign "quality weights" to health states in order to define measures of overall health, people are asked to express their preferences among diminished health states. For example, they might be asked to imagine that they face a choice between two life-saving operations, one of which will leave them unable to hear, the other unable to walk. (Both leave them with the same life expectancy.) Which do they prefer? Which would *you* prefer? How should people compare life without hearing to life without the use of their legs? By means of survey questions such as this one, health economists measure the "qualities" of health states needed to determine "quality-adjusted life years" (QALYs) or the disability weights needed to determine "disability-adjusted life years" (DALYs).[2]

Whether one would prefer to be deaf or confined to a wheel chair is a hard question that few survey respondents have thought about before. Moreover, it would be foolish for respondents to devote great effort to answering questions such as this one. The fact that people's answers to surveys are not based on extensive information, patient imagining, and careful reflection is a serious deficiency in such surveys, and it may be that the use of such surveys, like the reliance on contingent-valuation studies, reflects the pernicious influence of the misconception that preferences are just expressions of tastes. If instead of responding to a survey, this were a real question, it would be one of the most important decisions one would ever have to make, and most people would want to think hard before answering. They would seek out information concerning what it would be like to be unable to hear or unable to walk. They would try to imagine concretely what their lives would be like. They would want to know what careers they could pursue, what recreations they could engage in, how their families and friends would react. A good deal of self-knowledge would also be called for. I would ask myself what I most care about and what things I could most easily adapt to.

Both disabilities prevent people from doing things that most people value highly,[3] and depending on their values and circumstances, different people can justifiably defend different comparative evaluations. Jack may be justified in preferring to lose his hearing, while Jill is justified in preferring to lose her ability to walk. The right answer for Jack – what is, all things considered, better for him – may be the wrong answer for Jill. But what justifies preferences, and what makes preferences correct or incorrect?

---

[2] Because the use of QALYs or DALYs in assessment of the cost-effectiveness of health interventions or in determining summary measures of population health requires that these weights be quantitatively significant, respondents are in fact asked more difficult questions. For example, a survey used by the Institute for Health Metrics and Evaluation asks respondents which of the following they prefer. In the first scenario, "Imagine having 10 years left to live, and living for those ten years with the following health problems: You feel very weak, tired and short of breath, and you have problems with activities that require physical effort or deep concentration." In the second "Imagine having none of these problems or limitations but having only 7 years left to live." In my view, one should distinguish the question, "Which health state is better?" from the question "Which health state would you prefer?" but for the purposes of the discussion here, the differences can be ignored. For a sketch of how health states are evaluated and a critique of preference-based methods, see Hausman (2006).

[3] Which is not to say that either prevents individuals from living an excellent life. Disabilities such as these limit what kinds of lives people can live, not how good those lives can be.

Those faced with a choice between losing their hearing and losing their ability to walk need to figure out which health deficit is worse for them (or worse with respect to those things that they value most highly), and hence which they should prefer, not which they already prefer. Jack thus needs to think about how health deficiencies *matter*. Suppose that they matter to Jack, as to most people, in five main ways:

1. They affect people's feelings through physical sensations, such as pain or vertigo, and mental states, such as anxiety or depression.
2. They affect people's overall well-being.
3. They affect what projects and activities people can pursue and how successfully they can pursue them.
4. They affect the overall well-being of friends and family.
5. They affect the benefits that individuals provide to others and the burdens they impose on others.

Comparing deafness and paraplegia along these dimensions poses both factual and evaluative challenges, and one way that preferences can be unjustified or incorrect is if Jack makes factual mistakes about the consequences or characteristics of the two health states. Furthermore, even if Jack were able to make up his mind as to the comparative severity of deafness and paraplegia across each of the five dimensions, he would still face the problem of how to reach an overall judgment concerning which would be worse. Unless one is worse than the other with respect to all five aspects, Jack will need to consider the magnitude of the differences between the effects of deafness and paraplegia along each dimension and to place weights on the dimensions.

To carry out this task rationally, Jack needs to gather a good deal of information about the general consequences of paraplegia and deafness and the technological and personal resources available to those who cannot walk or who cannot hear. He needs to make inferences concerning the specific consequences for his own life from this general information and his knowledge of his circumstances, family, friends, abilities, habits, and personality. In addition to all this knowledge, Jack needs a healthy imagination, because to appreciate how he will feel, he needs to appreciate vividly what his life will be like (Egonsson 2007, pp. 152–53; Newell et al. 2007, p. 189). Jack will also need to rely heavily on his emotional reactions to how his life would change (Damasio 1994; but see also Elster 1999b, p. 159). As Elster points out, "Most simply, emotions matter because if we did not have them nothing else would matter [to us]" (1999a, p. 403).

Jack aims to come up with a comparative evaluation of deafness and paraplegia that is based on the facts and on the values of the attributes and consequences of deafness and paraplegia. In fact his evaluation depends on his beliefs, his evaluative attitudes, his imagination, and his emotions, any of which may mislead him about the facts or the values. Accordingly, there are four general ways in which Jack's comparative evaluation can be faulty either in the sense of reaching the wrong conclusion or in the sense of failing to reach its conclusion in a rationally defensible way:

1. The information Jack relies on may be false, or Jack may fail to gather relevant data or he may draw unjustified inferences from the data.
2. The values Jack relies on (which may themselves evolve in the course of his attempt to compare deafness and paraplegia) do not cohere with one another or with Jack's overall values. I say more about coherence in Section 10.6.
3. In imagining life with these disabilities, Jack may make mistakes. He might picture himself as a paraplegic sitting in a wheel chair, with his young daughter who wants to be carried upstairs to bed. As deaf, he might imagine himself sitting home alone unable to talk with his parents on the phone. These images will be painful, and his evaluation will be influenced by comparing how distressing these images are. But is he imagining his life as it actually would be? Because he is focusing on the health deficiencies, his images are likely to be a biased sample of snapshots of what his life would be like (Kahneman 1999, 2000a, 2000b; Gilbert 2006; Diener and Diener 2008). Jack is less likely to picture himself eating breakfast, reading a book, or watching a sunset, because these activities are not called to mind by thoughts of paraplegia and deafness. In addition, he may fail to imagine how he and his family and friends will adapt. As a paraplegic, he would be unlikely to be living in a multistory house without some sort of elevator, and if he were deaf, his parents would be accustomed to emailing or video-conferencing. Because he is reacting to a skewed set of images, his reactions are likely to lead him astray. On grounds such as these, one can criticize his imagining and hence his preferences.
4. Emotional reactions. Although Hume famously maintained that "Reason is, and ought only to be the slave of the passions" (1738, Book II, part III, sec. iii) and that it is incapable of assessing its masters, in fact emotions are subject to rational criticism, at least with respect to the judgments that they entail. For example, Jill is mistaken to be frightened by the fallen tree branch she thought to be a snake.

As this discussion has shown, there are many ways in which Jack's evaluation of deafness versus paraplegia can go awry, and hence many ways in which his preferences may be rationally indefensible and mistaken. Unsupported and false beliefs, skewed imagining, evaluative incoherence, and affective malfunction are all grounds for criticizing Jack's preferences. Preferences among health states are not mere matters of taste. They are not "the unchallengeable axioms of a man's behavior" "not capable of being changed by persuasion" (Stigler and Becker 1977, p. 76).

10.4. EMOTIONS AND RATIONAL EVALUATION

Comparative evaluation is a cognitive task. When trying to decide whether he prefers to lose his hearing or his ability to walk, Jack is not an explorer seeking in his feelings an answer to the question, "Which do I already prefer?" From a first-person perspective, Jack, like any other agent, cannot sensibly treat his preferences (construed as subjective evaluations) as facts about himself akin to facts about whether beans make him flatulent. Jack wants to know what reasons there are to judge deafness to be better or worse than paraplegia so that he will prefer the lesser deficiency. The task of comparative evaluation presents itself to agents as calling for judgment. Jack's question is, "Which is worse and more important to avoid?"

In addition to refining his beliefs concerning the characteristics and consequences of deafness and paraplegia, reflecting on his values and refining them, and exercising his imagination to make the alternatives vivid, Jack also needs emotional capacities to place weights on the states he imagines. As Ellen Peters points out, emotions play at least four roles in decision making:

1. Emotions are a source of information. "How do I or would I feel about this?"[4]
2. Emotions provide a common currency to compare alternatives.
3. Emotions focus the decision maker on new information that is then used in a second step used to guide choice.
4. Emotions motivate information processing and behavior. (Peters et al. 2006, pp. 80–81; Peters 2006, pp. 454–55)[5]

Emotions are bound to play a large role in empirical theories of evaluation such as consumer research. "[S]ome level of affect is necessary for information to have meaning so that decisions can be made" (Peters 2006, p. 463). But the place of emotions in normative theories is unclear. Insofar as emotions encapsulate past unconscious learning, they introduce nothing to the evaluation of alternatives beyond what an idealized model of rational deliberation would include. But ideally rational deliberation is not a serious option for human beings.

---

[4] As Lehrer points out, many of our emotions are fine-tuned by past experience and provide guidance concerning which states of affairs will meet our expectations. "Instead human emotions are rooted in predictions of highly flexible brain cells, which are constantly adjusting their connections to reflect reality. Every time you make a mistake or encounter something new, your brain cells are busy changing themselves. Our emotions are deeply empirical" (2009, p. 41).

[5] Emotions can also lead to bad choices and unjustified choices. Elster lists seven ways in which this may happen (1999a, pp. 285–86): (1) by biasing probabilities, (2) by biasing causal beliefs, (3) by inducing fantasy behavior (Sartre 1962), (4) by inducing painful fantasies, (5) by causing irrational behavior, (6) by creating a tendency to act precipitously, and (7) by inducing a disregard for consequences.

In my view, what defines emotions are three things: the action tendencies that emotions prompt, the feelings that are typical of them, and how the objects to which they respond bear on the interests of the person experiencing the emotion (Ben Ze'ev 2004; see also Damasio 1994; Elster 1999a, 1999b; Hastie and Dawes 2001, pp. 206f; Nussbaum 2001, 2004). For example, if Jill reacts to some event with grief, she is inclined to mourn, she feels upset, empty, diminished, and she believes that the event is a significant loss to her. According to Martha Nussbaum, "we are vulnerable to harm and damage in many ways.... Emotions are responses to these areas of vulnerability, responses in which we register the damages we have suffered, might suffer, or luckily have failed to suffer" (2004, p. 6). Specific emotions embody evaluative judgments concerning how states of affairs bear on our ends or goals and thus whether they are instances of what Anthony Kenny (1963) calls "the formal objects" of emotions. The formal objects of emotions partly define emotions. For example, the formal object of grief is a serious loss. To grieve at some state of affairs – some "material object" in Kenny's terminology – the agent must believe that it is an instance of the formal object – that is, that it involves the loss of something or someone of significant value to oneself. Nussbaum makes the stronger claim that grief "is *identical* with the acceptance of a proposition that is both evaluative and eudaimonistic, that is, concerned with one or more of the person's important goals and ends" (2001, p. 41 [my italics]). Although I believe that she (like Solomon 2003) exaggerates the cognitive component of emotion by *equating* emotions with the acceptance of judgments (Scarantino 2010), she is right to see judgments as essential to emotions, and the disagreements between her account and the one I am relying on do not bear on whether emotions are subject to rational criticism.

Emotional responses to events "are justified by what has happened, against the background of reasonable views about what matters" (Nussbaum 2004, p. 12). For an emotional reaction to be justified by what has happened or what one imagines to have happened, two conditions must be met. First, the agent is justified in taking the "material object" of the emotion – the state of affairs to which the agent is reacting – to be an instance of the emotion's formal object. Contentment is not a justified reaction to losing one's ability to walk, because losing one's ability to walk, unlike the formal object of contentment, is not something one wants and that gives pleasure. Second, people's reactions to the formal objects of emotions – to states of affairs that bear in particular ways on their interests – must be justified. Contentment should not lead to flight, nor should gratitude lead to aggression toward its object. If people form correct views about how states of affairs bear on their goals and interests and their reactions to states of affairs that bear in that way on their interests are justified, then the properties of states of affairs that cause their emotional reactions will also justify their reactions. Witnessing a beating justifies Jill's alarm and her retreat. Anticipation of a delicious meal justifies a pleasurable reaction and the pursuit of that meal. When one has learned how states of affairs bear on one's goals, how one should feel, and what one should be inclined to do, then emotions are justified: They are rationally defensible responses to their objects.

Emotional reactions are influenced by social norms. Cultures disagree about how states of affairs bear on people's goals and interests, about how people do and should feel when, for example, they have been insulted or benefitted, about what constitutes an insult or a benefit, and about how people do and should act in response to events that bear on their goals. So emotions will differ across societies.[6] Even those reactions that people acquire through their own experience are shaped by the reactions of others and the norms of their society. Having experienced the luxury of a warm bath, Jack reacts with pleasure to the thought of a warm bath. But he only experiences the bath as an innocent luxury (the formal object of a simple pleasure) in a society that does not regard nakedness as sinful. Emotional reactions carry the stamp of the society in which one lives and of one's experiences within that society.

In emphasizing the importance of social norms, I do not mean to suggest that social norms cannot be criticized nor that they automatically justify emotional reactions that accord with them. Just as people can acquire false and unjustified beliefs, so they may acquire unjustified emotional reactions. For example, not too long ago in the United States, a large portion of the population was repulsed by miscegenation and believed it to be unnatural. These beliefs and emotional reactions were indefensible. Statistical normality is only a rough guide to appropriate emotional reaction.

As illustrated by racist attitudes toward miscegenation or a simple case of someone terrified of dogs because she was bitten as a child, people can learn to react mistakenly just as they can learn to react correctly. In many cases, mistaken and unjustified reactions can be traced to unjustified or mistaken beliefs or to failures of imagination. In other cases, such as when Jill shrinks in terror from a dog that she knows to be harmless, there is a distortion in a person's affective faculties.[7] There are significant limits to the range of emotional reactions that are justified by what they are reactions to.

10.5. HUME'S CHALLENGE

The previous section argued that emotional reactions are subject to rational criticism. This conclusion faces a famous challenge from David Hume:

---

[6] Elster, in contrast, speculates that emotions are universal, although societies may fail to recognize them (1999b, p. 98). But if emotions are defined by beliefs about how states of affairs bear on human interests, about how people feel and act when states of affairs impinge on their lives, then they will differ from one society to another. These differences may, however, be small.

[7] One might argue that, despite knowing that the cocker spaniel in front of her is harmless, Jill has a persistent irrational belief in the dangers it poses which is embodied in her terror. Like Elster, I do not find this convincing (1999a, p. 117). See also Hunt 2006, p. 559.

A passion is an original existence, or, if you will, modification of existence, and contains not any representative quality, which renders it a copy of any other existence or modification. When I am angry, I am actually possest with the passion, and in that emotion have no more a reference to any other object, than when I am thirsty, or sick, or more than five foot high. `Tis impossible, therefore, that this passion can be opposed by, or be contradictory to truth and reason; since this contradiction consists in the disagreement of ideas, consider'd as copies, with those objects, which they represent.

Hume here maintains that *passions* do not represent anything. Like a feeling of nausea, a feeling of joy is not true or false or subject to rational criticism. Possessing no relation to any object, passions cannot be formed or modified by reason. Hume apparently denies that emotions rely on or entail beliefs.

But Hume then goes on:

[P]assions can be contrary to reason only so far as they are accompany'd with some judgment or opinion.... Where a passion is neither founded on false suppositions, nor chuses means insufficient for the end, the understanding can neither justify nor condemn it. `Tis not contrary to reason to prefer the destruction of the whole world to the scratching of my finger. It is not contrary to reason for me to chuse my total ruin, to prevent the least uneasiness of an Indian or person wholly unknown to me.... In short, a passion must be accompany'd with some false judgment in order to its being unreasonable; and even then `tis not the passion, properly speaking, which is unreasonable, but the judgment. (Hume 1738, Book II, part III, sec. iii.)

In this passage, Hume is mainly discussing "passions," although his most dramatic claims concern preference and choice. He maintains that passions are never "properly speaking" "unreasonable." If desires and emotional reactions were rushes of feelings that contingently accompany judgments, Hume would have a case. How could it be correct or mistaken, justified or unjustified for Jack to feel dizzy either when he whirls around or when he thinks about kissing Jill? But desires and emotions are not like vertigo. As Hume admits, passions may be "founded on" suppositions or judgments. Unlike feelings of dizziness, desires and emotions have objects.

Judgments concerning what has happened or will happen and how that bears on one's goals are partly constitutive of emotions. If Jill does not believe that she has suffered a loss, she may feel terrible, but her feeling is not grief. Whether or not her *feeling* is as objectless as Hume maintains, her *emotion* is not objectless, and it is hard to see how its evaluative force – the way in which it influences preferences – can arise from the feeling in isolation from the judgment the feeling is founded on.[8] Furthermore, Hume's claims about preferences do not follow from his view of feelings. Because the judgments that preferences presuppose concerning the characteristics and consequences of their objects may be false or unreasonable, Hume must concede that models

---

[8] For critiques of the Humean view, see Scanlon 1998 and Parfit 2011. For the best defense of a Humean view, see Schroeder 2007.

that show how final preferences among alternatives ought to depend on the evaluation of their attributes and consequences permit rational criticism of preferences. If the individual who prefers the destruction of the world to the scratching of her finger or who sacrifices what she knows to be vital to herself to provide a trivial benefit to someone else agrees with most people about the value of life, of pleasure, of beauty, and so forth, then her preferences will be in conflict with her values. If, in contrast, her beliefs and affective responses were reasonably coherent (which is hard to imagine), then there would be something badly wrong with her affective capacities.

Hume apparently agrees! In his essay, "On the Standard of Taste," he first restates his argument from the *Treatise*: "All sentiment is right; because sentiment has reference to nothing beyond itself, and is always real, wherever a man is conscious of it" (1741, p. 234). But then, speaking of the merits of Ogilby[9] and Bunyan compared to Addison and Milton, Hume writes, "Though there may be found persons, who give the preference to the former authors; no one pays attention to such a taste; and we pronounce, without scruple, the sentiment of these pretended critics to be absurd and ridiculous" (1741, p. 235).

If "all sentiment is right," how can some sentiments be "absurd and ridiculous"? Hume's answer is the following:

Some particular forms or qualities, from the original structure of the internal fabric are calculated to please, and others to displease; and if they fail of their effect in any particular instance, it is from some apparent defect or imperfection in this organ.... In each creature there is a sound and a defective state; and the former alone can be supposed to afford us a true standard of taste and sentiment. (1741, p. 238)

Tastes (and presumably passions and preferences) may be incorrect, even when there are no mistakes concerning matters of fact and no incoherence within an agent's affective states. If the "internal fabric" of those who prefer Ogilby to Milton is defective, then so are the evaluative capacities of someone who prefers to confer a trivial benefit on someone at the cost of his or her total ruin.

What Hume thought is not our main concern, since his views may be mistaken. His writings reveal a struggle to acknowledge the possibility of erroneous evaluation and the role of reason in evaluation without postulating objective values and human faculties to perceive them. I suspect that developments in psychology and neuroscience will corroborate hypotheses about defects in people's affective faculties. But even if they do not and theories of

---

[9] John Olgilby was a Scottish poet and geographer who lived from 1600 to 1676. The anonymous author of the 1822 *Lives of Scottish Poets* wrote of him, "The contempt which Pope, when of mature age, entertained for Ogilby's poetry and has expressed in the Dunciad, is repeated in still more explicit terms in the preface to his translation of the Iliad. It is there pronounced to be poetry too mean for criticism. I am sorry that I have nothing to oppose to so severe a sentence."

objective value come to naught, reason still has the four roles to play within evaluation listed in Section 10.3.

10.6. COHERENCE

In Section 10.3 I claimed that one of the ways in which Jack's comparative evaluation can be mistaken or unjustified is if his preferences are not coherent. Most commentators who have been concerned to evaluate preferences and choices have spoken instead of consistency and inconsistency. By inconsistency, they have meant both logical inconsistency, such as believing both *p* and not-*p*, and violations of axioms such as transitivity and context independence. One might, for example, call Morgenbesser's preference for apple pie when blueberry is the only alternative "inconsistent" with his preference for blueberry when he might have had apple or cherry. But such preferences violate no principles of logic.

It is less misleading to describe many of these failings as involving *incoherence* rather than inconsistency. Although coherence does not by itself constitute rationality (unless the acquisition of a novel passion for a person, cause, or activity, which disrupts a coherent set of attitudes, automatically counts as irrational), coherence is part of what constitutes rational agency. Part of rationality is manifesting some systematic unity in one's actions and attitudes. The demands of coherence among attitudes, desires, values, beliefs, and actions permit the development of additional theories of rational evaluation and preference formation.

Although there are no well-developed theories of evaluative coherence, I shall say a bit about what such theories should aim to do and how they should go about achieving their aims. Suppose that part of what it is to evaluate alternatives rationally is for those evaluations to cohere with each other and with one's emotions, attitudes, intentions, and beliefs. Following Paul Thagard (2000), let us model coherence as the satisfaction of a set of "constraints" that obtain among "elements." Elements consist of propositional attitudes. Positive constraints are ways in which pairs of elements cohere with one another. Negative constraints are ways in which pairs clash with one another. There are many specific constraints that may obtain among pairs of elements. For example, beliefs cohere when they bear entailment, explanatory, analogical, or conceptual relations to one another. There is a positive constraint between the belief that all humans are mortal and the belief that Michael Jackson died.

Coherence is then a matter of constraint satisfaction. Positive constraints between pairs of elements are satisfied if one accepts or rejects both elements. To satisfy a negative constraint, one accepts one of the elements and rejects the other. Weights can be assigned to constraints that correspond to their importance. There may also be noncoherence grounds for accepting or rejecting particular elements. In seeking coherence, an agent seeks to divide a set of elements into accepted and rejected sets in a way that satisfies the most constraints or the weightiest constraints. Thagard (2000) describes formal algorithms for determining the coherence among a set of representations.

Matters are complicated in the case of preferences in part because of the diversity of the elements among which one seeks coherence, consisting as they do of preferences, desires, values, beliefs, intentions, and emotions. In addition, the extent of coherence among preferences, desires, emotions, intentions, and values depends on an agent's beliefs. For example, if Jack believes that the liquid in the glass in front of him is water, then there is a positive constraint between Jack's desire for water and his intention to drink that liquid. If he believes instead that the liquid is rubbing alcohol, then there will be a negative constraint between the desire and the intention. One way to cope with this complication might be to determine first which beliefs cohere with one another and then to examine, conditional on those beliefs, the coherence between preferences, desires, intentions, and values. This is too simple, but it is one way to begin.

Although informative coherence models of preference formation and modification remain to be developed, their possibility defines further work for reason and further openings for the rational criticism and modification of preferences. For example, in construing strategic situations as games, players might be regarded as seeking a coherent view of their interactions. It may also be the case that some of the modeling tools developed by economists (especially concerning the determination of equilibria) can be put to work in assessing the constraint satisfaction and coherence of sets of beliefs and preferences.

Successful theories of rationally defensible emotional reaction and preference formation will, I believe, rely heavily on notions of coherence among emotions, judgments, feelings, and dispositions to act. Jill's fear of dogs is not justified because it does not cohere with her beliefs about the harmlessness of most dogs. Repugnance at miscegenation is not justified because it does not cohere with justified beliefs about the cultural and biological features of different races. Crucial to successful models of affective coherence will be an account of the relations between emotions and their formal and material objects and between emotions and practices. This suggestion, however, is only a promissory note, because I have not formulated any theory of affective coherence.

10.7. CONCLUSION: THEORIES OF PREFERENCE FORMATION

To maintain that preferences are subject to rational criticism is not to maintain that there is some unique set of rational preferences for any individual. On the same evidence, Jack and Jill may sometimes justifiably reach different conclusions. They may imagine alternatives in different rationally defensible ways. And their emotional reactions may differ to some extent without either being unjustified. An account of rational evaluation permits a range of different preferences.

The goal of this chapter has been to give substance to the claim that preferences are subject to rational appraisal and that preference formation is a subject for economic modeling. Preferences can be criticized as based on false beliefs, as incoherent, or as driven by distorted imagination or unjustified emotional reactions. Even a Humean view of desires permits this sort of rational scrutiny of preferences.

A theory that deduces choices from constraints, beliefs, and preferences requires that, given beliefs, preferences *determine* choices. The cost of this simplicity in the connection between preferences and choice is complexity in the determination of preferences. Merely specifying formal conditions on preferences, even if they were satisfied, does not permit economists to predict or explain anything. Economists need to know how people value the consequences or attributes of alternatives and how those values determine (final) preferences among the immediate objects of choice. To meet this need, economists rely, on the one hand, on a consequentialist view of preference formation and, on the other hand, on simple generalizations such as that people prefer larger commodity bundles to smaller. But these generalizations are rarely accurate or detailed enough to predict what people will do.

There is no need to insist that generalizations such as nonsatiation are the only substantive things economists can say about agent's preferences. Hedonic pricing models permit more specific generalizations about what determines demand for specific commodities and services. While retaining a view of preferences as transitive and choice-determining, one can help oneself to a panoply of generalizations concerning the ways in which preferences depend on the attributes of alternatives, as well as on the context, the mode of elicitation, heuristics, fashions, loyalties, or social norms. In some contexts, it may be a good approximation to suppose that people care only about their own financial returns or the size of their consumption bundles; in such contexts, standard economic models can be very useful. In other contexts, people's own financial returns or the quantities of commodities may be relatively minor factors influencing preferences. Good theories of how people form and modify their preferences will not be simple.

Although not simple, useful models of preference formation are not beyond the economic pale. Economists are already committed to consequentialist models of preference formation. As the literature on hedonic pricing shows, formulating finer-grained models of the factors influencing preferences does not require a completely different kind of enterprise. Moreover, as this chapter has argued, the view that preferences are not subject to rational criticism is untenable even from a narrow Humean perspective.

Economics is not a theory of rationally consistent fools who mindlessly manage to choose in accordance with a predetermined complete, transitive, and context-independent ranking. Although some economists may mistakenly claim that preferences are impervious to rational criticism or that they reflect relentless self-interest, the concept of preferences that economists do and should employ does not commit them to such indefensible views. All it commits them to is regarding preferences as total subjective evaluations and hence as choice-determining. It thereby structures their explanations and predictions and permits shaky inferences concerning welfare while creating a space for models of how preferences are and should be formed and modified.

11

Conclusions

I began by distinguishing four conceptions of preference: favoring, enjoyment comparison, choice ranking, and comparative evaluation, which may be total, as in economics, or "overall" and hence partial, as in everyday usage. In taking preferences to be complete and stable, economists are often inclined to regard questions about their provenance and modification as outside of the purview of economics and indeed as beyond rational scrutiny. They are tempted to think of preferences as mere matters of taste. These views were repeatedly criticized. Enjoyment comparisons, in contrast to total comparative evaluations, do not determine choices and for that reason cannot constitute the concept of preferences that economists employ. Nor (as argued in Chapter 3) will preferences defined by choices serve the purposes of economists, because such preferences only rank the immediate objects of choice and their relation to choice is independent of belief.

As argued in the first six chapters, the concept of preferences as comparative evaluations is central to positive economics as well as to much of everyday talk concerning preferences. Experimental demonstrations of the volatility of preferences discussed in Chapter 9 show that social scientists have to choose between taking preferences to be total but context-dependent evaluations (which is the view I have defended) and taking preferences to be stable but only partial evaluations that compete with other factors in the determination of choices.

Social scientists face strategic choices concerning how to model human behavior. Should they make use of a concept of preferences (as comparative evaluation) and should they take these comparative evaluations to be total or partial? Economists have chosen to structure their inquiries around a notion of preferences as total comparative evaluations: All the factors that influence choices (apart from constraints and beliefs) affect choices *via* their influence on preferences. Coupled with beliefs and constraints, preferences *determine* choices. As discussed in Chapter 6, this is not the only way to conceive of preferences, but, as mainstream positive economics and game theory demonstrate,

133

there are major advantages to maintaining a tight linkage between preferences and choices and addressing the complexities of evaluation and deliberation within an account of preference formation and modification rather than within a theory in which preferences compete with other factors to determine choices. This modeling choice fixes a concept of preferences as transitive, choice-determining, and, with respect to the characteristics and consequences of choices, complete. Economists would like to treat preferences as context-independent as well, but, as the evidence shows, preferences systematically depend on features of the context such as the mode of elicitation and the specification of a reference point. Context dependence, heuristics, and deliberative flaws open the door to failures of rationality and create a gulf between theories of actual and rational choice. This gulf may be regrettable, but methodological longing cannot make the theory of rational choice into an accurate account of actual choice.

Self-interest obviously influences preferences. People often prefer one alternative x to another alternative y because they believe that x is better for them than y is. For this reason, it is often sensible to take people's preferences as guides to what benefits them – at least with respect to alternatives whose attributes and consequences they understand well. But there are few people who do not distinguish between "What should I prefer – that is, what is overall best?" and "What is best for me?" Even fewer do not have some mistaken beliefs concerning the character and consequences of the alternatives they are evaluating. Moreover, preferences are sensitive to context, often constructed on the fly, and distorted by heuristics and flaws in deliberation. Economists cannot read off what is good for people from what they choose.

The cure for these problems with normative economics, like the cure for the predictive limitations of the standard model of choice, is to understand more clearly what preferences are and to pay closer attention to the factors that influence preferences. There are many:

- Beliefs concerning consequences and characteristics of alternatives; information processing and inferential abilities.
- Tastes, longings, emotions, likes and dislikes, and experiences and anticipations of enjoyment.
- Ideals, objectives, personal commitments, identifications, and conceptions of oneself.
- Contextually determined reference points or anchors and decision-making heuristics.
- Physiological needs, imaginative capacities, psychological mechanisms including cognitive flaws such as overconfidence, exaggerated optimism, status quo bias, inertia, inattention, myopia, conformity, akrasia, and addiction.
- Social factors such as norms and laws, and the wishes, examples and arguments of others.

Because these influences are diverse and interact, the prospects for a unified theory of preference formation are bleak. But useful theories can have narrow scope. Narrowly focused models of preference formation and modification are already in use.

Misconceptions concerning preferences have stood in the way of modeling preference formation and have impeded progress in both positive and normative economics. Chapter 1 listed five misconceptions:

1. *Arbitrariness*: As argued in Chapters 2, 6, 8, and 10, economists should not assimilate preferences to tastes or comparative enjoyment, concerning which rational criticism is impossible. Not only is this view of preferences at odds with the axioms, but conceiving of preferences this way leads to mistakes, such as the surveys of health preferences mentioned in Chapter 10 or some contingent valuation studies. Thinking of preferences as nothing more than tastes also discourages inquiry into the sources of preferences. Preferences are total comparative evaluations, which are more like judgments than feelings.

2. *Self-interest*: As argued in Chapters 2 and 8, preferences are not exclusively self-interested and cannot be defined by self-interest. When deciding what to do, people are not always thinking about their own interests, nor do they always put their own interests first. This misconception does real harm by leading economists to exaggerate the connection between welfare and preference satisfaction. The use of contingent valuation studies to quantify the value of preserving endangered species or environments reflects the misconception that people's preferences always correspond to their beliefs about what will benefit them.

3. *Revealed preference*: As argued in Chapter 3, preferences cannot be defined in terms of actual or hypothetical choice. Even final preferences do not result in choices without the intermediary of belief. It is, however, not clear how much damage revealed-preference theory does, because much of what is called "revealed-preference theory" is not committed to this mistaken conception of preference.

4. *Division of theoretical labor*: As argued in Chapters 4, 5, 6, and 10, economists do and should model preference formation and modification. Economic models make substantive claims about the content of preferences, and expected-utility theory, multi-attribute utility theory, and game theory all provide consequentialist models of preference formation. The view that economists have nothing to say about preference formation has prevented economists from appreciating how deeply engaged they already are in theorizing about what influences preferences, and it has impeded work on preference formation.

5. *Welfare as preference satisfaction*: As argued in Chapter 7, the satisfaction of preferences does not constitute welfare. Preferences are total comparative evaluations, not partial evaluations in terms of expected

benefit, and even when self-interested, preferences may be mistaken. Much of welfare economics can be salvaged, because preferences are often good evidence concerning what makes people better off. But understanding that preference satisfaction does not constitute welfare shifts the focus from preference satisfaction per se to drawing inferences concerning what is good for people. Without understanding when satisfying preferences does not contribute to welfare, cost-benefit analysis and other techniques of welfare economics may be misapplied.

Correcting these misconceptions does not require that economists burn their books and start over. Even though preferences are central to mainstream economics, the precise interpretation of preferences is sometimes of little importance. As I just argued, these misconceptions have harmed some parts of economics, but the harm is localized, and the misconceptions are relatively easy to correct. Cost-benefit analysis does not need to be abandoned, although its scope must be narrowed, and in some cases economists should be more concerned with people's expectations of benefit than with their preferences. Recognizing the context dependence of preferences does not render consumer choice theory worthless, but it does call for greater caution in its application. Rather than suggesting any errors within game theory, the argument of Chapters 5 and 6 points to the need to supplement game theory with systematic inquiry into how agents confronting a strategic interaction construct the game they play.

Although it criticizes misconceptions concerning preferences, this book has, I hope, a constructive message. Conceiving of preferences explicitly as subjective total comparative evaluations enables social scientists to define a general model of choice behavior ("the standard model"), in which choices are determined by constraints, beliefs, and final preferences. In employing the standard model, economists need not portray agents as rational fools. They need not deny that many different things influence choices. All that economists need to insist on is that other influences on choices, such as emotions, imagination, or social norms, do so by influencing constraints, beliefs, or preferences. Having done this, they should inquire about how these other factors influence preferences. In many cases, the behavioral generalizations and analytic techniques of economics will be of little help in understanding how preferences are formed, and the view that questions about preference formation are best left to other social scientists will have some justification. But once economists clearly understand that they rely on a conception of preferences as subjective total comparative evaluations and hence as the outcomes of a deliberative process – albeit certainly not a passionless or ideally rational one – then economists can see the challenges and opportunities they face in modeling aspects of that process. Conceiving of preferences as total comparative evaluations also enables social scientists concerned with measuring and increasing welfare to recognize that preferences can be a fallible guide to welfare.

Knowing that my son, at age three, preferred a career as an "aphosopher," a gravel-truck driver, or as a horseback hunter permitted some predictions about his behavior at that time, even though he did not yet face a career choice. Knowing these preferences was informative, because they were linked to more general dispositions, likes, and dislikes. So, predictably, he liked to ask puzzling questions. ("Why birds?" was, I recall, a stumper.) He was thrilled with his Fisher-Price yellow plastic gravel truck with its precious plastic driver. And although deprived of horseback riding and guns, he was as active and mobile as Wild Bill Hickok. As a guide to his welfare, on the other hand, his preferences were at that age of lesser value. He had a great deal to learn about adult life and his own capacities and interests. It never occurred to my wife or to me to structure his upbringing so as to bring about one of his favored three career choices, and we do not believe that by failing to do so we made him less well off than he otherwise would have been.

The vulgar view of people as "rational fools," against which Sen so eloquently complains, is not an unavoidable consequence of modeling choices as determined by constraints, beliefs, and preferences. If one interprets preferences correctly as subjective total comparative evaluations, then one can understand that models that explain and predict choices in terms of preferences and beliefs regiment folk psychology by sharpening the relationship between choices and preferences and by quarantining many hard questions within accounts of preference formation and modification. This regimentation has its drawbacks, but – or so this book has argued – it has many advantages, too.

References

Adler, Matthew and Eric Posner. 2006. *New Foundations of Cost-Benefit Analysis.* Cambridge, MA: Harvard University Press.

Alvard, Michael. 2004. "The Ultimatum Game, Fairness, and Cooperation among Big Game Hunters." *Foundations of Human Sociality* 39: 413–51.

Amir, On, Orly Lobel, and Dan Ariely. 2005. "Making Consumption Decisions by Following Personal Rules." In Ratneshwar and David Mick, eds., pp. 86–101.

Anderson, Elizabeth. 2001. "Unstrapping the Straitjacket of 'Preference': A Comment on Amartya Sen's Contributions to Philosophy and Economics." *Economics and Philosophy* 17: 21–38.

Arneson, Richard. 1990. "Liberalism, Distributive Subjectivism, and Equal Opportunity for Welfare." *Philosophy & Public Affairs* 19: 158–94.

Arrow, Kenneth. 1951. *Social Choice and Individual Values.* New Haven, CT: Yale University Press.

1959. "Rational Choice Functions and Ordering." *Economica* 26: 121–27.

1970. *Essays in the Theory of Risk Bearing.* Amsterdam: North Holland.

1973. "Some Ordinalist-Utilitarian Notes on Rawls' Theory of Justice." *Journal of Philosophy* 70: 246–63.

Arrow, Kenneth, Robert Solow, Paul Portney, Edward Leamer, Roy Radner, and Howard Schuman. 1993. "Report of the NOAA Panel on Contingent Valuation." *Federal Register* 58(10), 4601–14.

Bagozzi, Richard, Hans Baumgartner, Rik Pieters, and Marcel Zeelenberg. 2000. "The Role of Emotions in Goal-Directed Behavior." In Ratneshwar, Mick, and Huffman, eds., pp. 36–58.

Belk, Russell. 1988. "Possessions and the Extended Self." *The Journal of Consumer Research* 15: 139–68.

Bell, David, Ralph Keeney, and Howard Raiffa, eds. 1977. *Conflicting Objectives in Decisions.* New York: John Wiley & Sons.

Ben-Ze'ev, Aaron. 2004. "Emotions Are Not Mere Judgments." *Philosophy and Phenomenological Research* 68: 450–57.

Bicchieri, Cristina. 2005. *The Grammar of Society: The Nature and Dynamics of Social Norms.* Cambridge, Cambridge University Press.

Binmore, Ken. 1994. *Playing Fair.* Cambridge, MA: MIT Press.

Blount, Sally. 1995. "When Social Outcomes Aren't Fair: The Effect of Causal Attributions on Preferences." *Organizational Behavior and Human Decision Processes* 63: 131–44.

Boardman, Anthony, David Greenberg, Aidan Vining, and David Weimer. 2010. *Cost-Benefit Analysis*. 4th ed. Englewood Cliffs, NJ: Prentice-Hall.

Border, Kim. 1992. "Revealed Preference, Stochastic Dominance, and the Expected Utility Hypothesis." *Journal of Economic Theory* 56: 20–42.

Brandt, Richard. 1979. *A Theory of the Right and the Good*. Oxford: Oxford University Press.

1998. "The Rational Criticism of Preferences." In Fehige and Wessels, eds., pp. 62–77.

Bratman, Michael. 1987. *Intention, Plans, and Practical Reason*. Cambridge, MA: Harvard University Press.

1999. *Faces of Intention: Selected Essays on Intention and Agency*. Cambridge: Cambridge University Press.

2007a. *Structures of Agency*. Oxford: Oxford University Press.

2007b. "Valuing and the Will." In Bratman 2007a, pp. 47–67.

Broadway, Robin and Neil Bruce. 1984. *Welfare Economics*. Oxford: Basil Blackwell.

Broome, John. 1991a. "Utility." *Economics and Philosophy* 7: 1–12.

1991b. *Weighing Goods*. Oxford: Basil Blackwell.

Bykvist, Krister. 2010. "Can Unstable Preferences Provide a Stable Standard of Well-Being?" *Economics and Philosophy* 26: 1–26.

Camerer, Colin, Samuel Issacharoff, George Loewenstein, Ted O'Donoghue, and Matthew Rabin. 2003. "Regulation for Conservatives: Behavioral Economics and the Case for Asymmetric Paternalism." *University of Pennsylvania Law Review* 151: 1211–54.

Caplin, Andrew and Andrew Schotter, eds. 2008. *Handbook of Economic Methodology*. Oxford: Oxford University Press.

Chapman, Bruce. 2003. "Rational Choice and Categorical Reason." *University of Pennsylvania Law Review* 151: 1169–210.

Chu, Y. and R. Chu. 1990. "The Subsidence of Preference Reversals in Simplified and Marketlike Experimental Settings: A Note." *American Economic Review* 80: 902–11.

Churchland, Paul. 1981. "Eliminative Materialism and the Propositional Attitudes." *Journal of Philosophy* 78: 67–90.

Crisp, R. 2006. *Reasons and the Good*. Oxford: Oxford University Press.

Damasio, A. R. 1994. *Descartes' Error: Emotion, Reason, and the Human Brain*. New York: Avon.

Danto, Arthur. 1973. *Analytical Philosophy of Action*. Cambridge: Cambridge University Press.

Davidson, Donald. 1963. "Actions, Reasons, and Causes." *Journal of Philosophy* 60: 685–700.

1980. *Essays on Actions and Events*. Oxford: Oxford University Press.

2004. *Problems of Rationality*. Oxford: Oxford University Press.

Debreu, Gerard. 1959. *Theory of Value: An Axiomatic Analysis of Economic Equilibrium*. New York: John Wiley & Sons.

Diener, Ed and Robert Diener. 2008. *Happiness: Unlocking the Mysteries of Psychological Wealth*. New York: Wiley-Blackwell.

Dinan, Terry and David Austin. 2004. "Fuel Economy Standards versus a Gasoline Tax." *Congressional Budget Office*.

Dolan, Paul and Daniel Kahneman. 2008. "Interpretations of Utility and Their Implications for the Valuation of Health." *Economic Journal* 118: 215–34.

Dretske, Fred. 1991. *Explaining Behavior: Reasons in a World of Causes*. Cambridge, MA: MIT Press.

Dworkin, Gerald. 1971. "Paternalism." In Richard Wasserstrom (ed.), *Morality and the Law*. Belmont: Wadsworth, pp. 107–36.

Dworkin, Ronald. 1981. "What Is Equality? Part 2: Equality of Resources." *Philosophy & Public Affairs* 10: 283–385.

Eells, Ellery. 1982. *Rational Decision and Causality*. Cambridge: Cambridge University Press.

Egonsson, Dan. 2007. *Preference and Information*. Aldershot, Hampshire: Ashgate Publishing.

Elster, Jon. 1983. *Sour Grapes: Studies in the Subversion of Rationality*. Cambridge: Cambridge University Press.

1999a. *Alchemies of the Mind: Rationality and the Emotions*. Cambridge: Cambridge University Press.

1999b. *Strong Feelings: Emotion, Addition, and Human Behavior*. Cambridge, MA: MIT Press.

Elster, Jon and Aanund Hylland, eds. 1986. *Foundations of Social Choice Theory*. Cambridge: Cambridge University Press.

Enç, Berent. 2006. *How We Act: Causes, Reasons and Intentions*. Oxford: Oxford University Press.

Fankhauser, Samuel, Richard Tol, and David Pearce. 1997. "The Aggregation of Climate Change Damages: A Welfare Theoretic Approach." *Environmental and Resource Economics* 10: 249–66.

Fehige, Christoph and Ulla Wessels, eds. 1998. *Preferences*. New York: Walter de Gruyter.

Fehr, Ernst and Klaus Schmidt. 1999. "A Theory of Fairness, Competition, and Cooperation." *Quarterly Journal of Economics* 114: 817–68.

Feldman, F. 2004. *Pleasure and the Good Life: Concerning the Nature, Varieties, and Plausibility of Hedonism*. Oxford: Oxford University Press.

Fishburn, Peter. 1977. "Multiattribute Utilities in Expected Utility Theory." In Bell, Keeney, and Raiffa, eds., pp. 172–96.

Fisher, R.A. 1959. *Smoking – The Cancer Controversy*. Edinburgh: Oliver and Boyd.

Fournier, Susan. 1998. "Consumers and Their Brands: Developing Relationship Theory in Consumer Research." *Journal of Consumer Research* 24: 343–73.

Frank, Robert. 1987. *Choosing the Right Pond: Human Behavior and the Quest for Status*. Oxford: Oxford University Press.

2000. "Why Is Cost-Benefit Analysis So Controversial?" *Journal of Legal Studies* 29: 913–30.

Frank, Robert and Phillip Cook. 1996. *The Winner-Take-All Society: Why the Few at the Top Get So Much More Than the Rest of Us*. New York: Penguin Books.

Frankfurt, Harry. 1971. "Freedom of Will and the Concept of a Person." *Journal of Philosophy* 68: 5–20.

Frey, Bruno. 2010. *Happiness: A Revolution in Economics*. Cambridge, MA: MIT Press.

Frey, Bruno and Alois Stutzer. 2001. *Happiness and Economics: How the Economy and Institutions Affect Human Well-Being*. Princeton, NJ: Princeton University Press.

Gauthier, David. 1986. *Morals by Agreement*. Oxford: Oxford University Press.

Gibbard, Alan. 1986. "Interpersonal Comparisons: Preference, Good, and the Intrinsic Reward of a Life." In Elster and Hylland (1986), pp. 165–94.

1998 "Preferences and Preferability." In Fehige and Wessels, eds., pp. 239–59.

Gibbard, Alan and William Harper. 1978. "Counterfactuals and Two Kinds of Expected Utility." In William Harper, Robert Stalnaker and Glen Pearce, eds., *Ifs*. Dordrecht: Reidel, pp. 153–90.

Gilbert, Daniel. 2006. *Stumbling on Happiness*. New York: Knopf.

Glimcher, Paul, Colin Camerer, Russell Poldrack, and Ernst Fehr, eds. 2009. *Neuroeconomics: Decision Making and the Brain*. Amsterdam: Elsevier.

Goodin, Robert. 1986. "Laundering Preferences." In Elster and Hylland (1986), pp. 75–101.

Gravell, Hugh and Ray Rees. 1981. *Microeconomics*. London: Longmans.

Green, Edward and Kent Osbard. 1991. "A Revealed Preference Theory for Expected Utility." *Review of Economic Studies* 58: 677–96.

Grether, David and Charles Plott. 1979. "Economic Theory of Choice and the Preference Reversal Phenomenon." *American Economic Review* 69: 623–38.

Griffin, James. 1986. *Well-Being: Its Meaning, Measurement and Moral Importance*. Oxford: Clarendon Press.

1996. *Value Judgement: Improving our Ethical Beliefs*. Oxford: Oxford University Press.

Grüne-Yanoff, Till and Sven Hansson, eds. 2007. *Preference Change: Approaches from Philosophy, Economics and Psychology*. Dordrecht: Springer.

Gul, Faruk and Wolfgang Pesendorfer. 2008. "The Case for Mindless Economics." In Caplin and Schotter, eds., pp. 3–39.

Hammond, Peter. 1983. "Ex-Post Optimality as a Dynamically Consistent Objective for Collective Choice under Uncertainty." In P. Pattanaik and M. Salles, eds., *Social Choice and Welfare*. Amsterdam: North-Holland.

1988a. "Consequentialism and the Independence Axiom." In B. Munier, ed., *Risk, Decision and Rationality*. Dordrecht: Reidel, pp. 503–16.

1988b. "Consequentialist Foundations for Expected Utility." *Theory and Decision* 25: 25–78.

Hansson, Sven and Till Grüne-Yanoff. 2006. "Preferences." *Stanford Encyclopedia of Philosophy*. http://plato.stanford.edu/entries/preferences/

Harris, R. and N. Olewiler. 1979. "The Welfare Economics of *ex post* Optimality." *Economica* 46: 137–47.

Harsanyi, John. 1977. *Rational Behavior and Bargaining Equilibrium in Games and Social Situations*. Cambridge: Cambridge University Press.

Hastie, Reid and Robyn Dawes. 2001. *Rational Choice in an Uncertain World*. Thousand Oaks, CA: Sage Publications.

Hausman, Daniel. 1995. "The Impossibility of Interpersonal Utility Comparisons." *Mind* 104: 473–90.

2000. "Revealed Preference, Belief, and Game Theory." *Economics and Philosophy* 16: 99–116.

2005a. "Sympathy, Commitment, and Preference." *Economics and Philosophy* 21: 33–50; Rpt. in Fabienne Peter and Hans Bernhard Schmid, eds. *Rationality and Commitment*. Oxford: Oxford University Press, 2008, pp. 49–69.

2005b. "Testing Game Theory." *Journal of Economic Methodology* 12: 211–23.

2006a. "Valuing Health." *Philosophy and Public Affairs* 34: 246–74.

2006b. "Consequentialism, and Preference Formation in Economics and Game Theory." *Philosophy* 59 (Supplement): 111–29.

2007. "The Philosophical Foundations of Mainstream Normative Economics." *The Philosophy of Economics: An Anthology* (3rd edition) (co-authored with Michael McPherson). Cambridge: Cambridge University Press, pp. 226–50.

2008a. "Fairness and Social Norms." *Philosophy of Science* 75(5): 850–60.

2008b. "Mindless or Mindful Economics: A Methodological Evaluation." In Caplin and Schotter, eds., pp. 125–51.

2009. "Rational Preference and Evaluation." *Occasion: Interdisciplinary Studies in the Humanities* 1(1), http://occasion.stanford.edu/node/21

2010. "Valuing Health: A New Proposal." *Health Economics* 19: 280–96.

2011. "Mistakes about Preferences in the Social Sciences." *Philosophy of the Social Sciences* 41: 3–25.

Hausman, Daniel and Michael McPherson. 1994. "Preference, Belief, and Welfare." *American Economic Review Papers and Proceedings* 84: 396–400.

2006. *Economic Analysis, Moral Philosophy, and Public Policy*. Cambridge: Cambridge University Press.

2009. "Preference Satisfaction and Welfare Economics," *Economics and Philosophy* 25: 1–25.

Hausman, Daniel and Brynn Welch. 2010. "To Nudge or Not to Nudge." *Journal of Political Philosophy* 18: 123–36.

Heathwood, C. 2005. "The Problem of Defective Desires." *Australasian Journal of Philosophy* 83: 487–504.

Henderson, James and Richard Quandt. 1980. *Microeconomic Theory: A Mathematical Approach*. 3rd ed. New York: McGraw-Hill.

Hicks, John. 1939. "The Foundations of Welfare Economics." *Economic Journal* 49: 696–712.

Hitchcock, Christopher. 1996. "Causal Decision Theory and Decision-Theoretic Causation." *NOUS* 30: 508–26.

Holt, Douglas. 2005. "How Societies Desire Brands: Using Cultural Theory to Explain Brand Symbolism." In Ratneshwar and David Mick, eds., pp. 273–91.

Houtthaker, H. 1950. "Revealed Preference and the Utility Function." *Economica* 17: 159–74.

Hume, David. 1738. *A Treatise of Human Nature*. Rpt. 2000. Oxford: Oxford University Press.

1741. "Of the Standard of Taste." In *Essays, Moral, Political and Literary*. Rpt. 1963. Oxford: Oxford University Press.

Hunt, Lester. 2006. "Martha Nussbaum on the Emotions." *Ethics* 116: 552–77.

Jeffrey, Richard. 1983. *The Logic of Decision*. 2nd ed. Chicago: University of Chicago Press.

Joyce, James. 1999. *The Foundations of Causal Decision Theory*. Cambridge: Cambridge University Press.

Kahneman, Daniel. 1999. "Objective Happiness." In D. Kahneman, E. Diener and N. Schwarz, eds., *Well-Being: Foundations of Hedonic Psychology*. New York: Russell Sage Foundation Press, pp. 3–27.

2000a. "Evaluation by Moments: Past and Future." In Kahneman and Tversky, eds., pp. 693–708.

2000b. "Experienced Utility and Objective Happiness: A Moment-based Approach." In Kahneman and Tversky, eds., pp. 673–92.

Kahneman, Daniel, Jack L. Knetsch, and Richard H. Thaler. 1991. "The Endowment Effect, Loss Aversion, and Status Quo Bias." *The Journal of Economic Perspectives*, 5: 193–206.

Kahneman, Daniel and Alan Krueger. 2006. "Developments in the Measurement of Subjective Well Being." *Journal of Economic Perspectives* 20: 3–24.

Kahneman, Daniel and Richard Thaler. 2006. "Utility Maximization and Experienced Utility." *Journal of Economic Perspectives* 20: 221–34.

Kahneman, Daniel and Amos Tversky. 1979. "Prospect Theory." *Econometrica* 47: 263–91.

Kahneman, Daniel and Amos Tversky, eds. 2000. *Choices, Values and Frames*. New York: Cambridge University Press and the Russell Sage Foundation.

Kaldor, Nicholas. 1939. "Welfare Propositions of Economics and Interpersonal Comparisons of Utility." *Economic Journal* 49: 549–52.

Keeney, Ralph. 1982. "Decision Analysis: An Overview." *Operations Research* 30: 803–38.

1992. *Value-Focused Thinking: A Path to Creative Decisionmaking*. Cambridge, MA: Harvard University Press.

Keeney, Ralph and Howard Raiffa. 1993. *Decisions with Multiple Objectives: Preferences and Value Tradeoffs*. 2nd ed. Cambridge: Cambridge University Press.

Kenney, Anthony. 1963. *Actions, Emotion and Will*. London: Routledge.

Kraut, Richard. 2007. *What Is Good and Why*. Cambridge, MA: Harvard University Press.

Kremer, Michael, Edward Miguel, Jessica Leino, and Alix Peterson Zwane. 2011. "Spring Cleaning: Rural Water Impacts, Valuation, and Property Rights Institutions." *Quarterly Journal of Economics* 126: 145–205.

Lancaster, Kelvin. 1966. "A New Approach to Consumer Theory." *Journal of Political Economy* 74: 132–57.

1979. *Variety, Equity, and Efficiency*. New York: Columbia University Press.

Layard, Richard. 2006. *Happiness: Lessons from a New Science*. New York: Penguin.

Layard, Richard and Stephen Glaister. 1994. "Introduction." In Richard Layard and Stephen Glaister, eds., *Cost-Benefit Analysis*. 2nd ed. Cambridge: Cambridge University Press, pp. 1–56.

Le Grand, Julian. 1991. *Equity and Choice: An Essay in Economics and Applied Philosophy*. London: Harper-Collins.

Lehrer, Jonah. 2009. *How We Decide*. New York: Houghton Mifflin Harcourt.

Lewis, David. 1981. "Causal Decision Theory." *Australasian Journal of Philosophy* 59: 5–30.

Lichtenstein, Sarah and Paul Slovic. 1971. "Reversals of Preferences between Bids and Choices in Gambling Decisions." *Journal of Experimental Psychology* 89: 46–55.

1973. "Response-Induced Reversals of Preference in Gambling: An Extended Replication in Las Vegas." *Journal of Experimental Psychology* 101: 16–20.

Lichtenstein, Sarah and Paul Slovic, eds. 2006a. *The Construction of Preference*. New York: Cambridge University Press.

2006b. "The Construction of Preference: An Overview." In Lichtenstein and Slovic, eds., pp. 1–49.

Litt, Ron, Chris Eliasmith, and Paul Thagard. 2009. "Neural Affective Decision Theory: Choices, Brains, and Emotions." *Cognitive Systems Research* 9: 252–73.

Little, I. M. D. 1949. "A Reformulation of the Theory of Consumers' Behaviour." *Oxford Economic Papers* 1: 90–99.

Loewenstein, George. 2007. *Exotic Preferences: Behavioral Economics and Human Motivation*. Oxford: Oxford University Press.

Loewenstein, George and E. Angner. 2003. "Predicting and Indulging Changing Preferences." In G. Loewenstein, D. Read, and R. Baumeister, eds., *Time and Decision: Economic and Psychological Perspectives on Intertemporal Choice*. New York: Russell Sage Foundation, pp. 351–91.

Malpezzi, Stephen. 2002. "Hedonic Pricing Models: A Selective and Applied Review." In Tony O'Sullivan and Kenneth Gibb, eds., *Housing Economics and Public Policy*. Oxford: Blackwell, pp. 67–89.

Mas-Colell, Andreu, Michael Whinston, and Jerry Green. 1995. *Microeconomic Theory*. New York: Oxford University Press.

McClennen, Edward. 1990. *Rationality and Dynamic Choice: Foundational Explorations*. Cambridge: Cambridge University Press.

McKerlie, Dennis. 2007. "Rational Choice, Changes in Values over Time and Well-Being." *Utilitas* 19: 51–72.

Mele, Alfred R., ed. 1997. *Philosophy of Action*. Oxford: Oxford University Press.

Mongin, Philippe. 2000. "Les Préférences Révélées et la Formation de la Théorie du Consommateur." *Revue Economique* 51: 1125–52.

Muniz, Albert, Jr. and Thomas O'Guinn. 2001. "Brand Community." *Journal of Consumer Research* 27: 412–31.

Nagel, Thomas. 1986. *The View from Nowhere*. New York: Oxford University Press.

Nelson, Paul. 1999. "Multiattribute Utility Models." In Peter Earl and Simon Kemp, eds., *Elgar Companion to Consumer Research and Economic Psychology*. Cheltenham: Edward Elgar, pp. 392–400.

Newell, Benjamin, David Lagnado, and David Shanks. 2007. *Straight Choices: The Psychology of Decision Making*. New York: Psychology Press.

Nozick, Robert. 1974. *Anarchy, State, and Utopia*. New York: Basic Books.

Nussbaum, Martha. 2001. *Upheavals of Thought: The Intelligence of Emotions*. Cambridge: Cambridge University Press.

2004. *Hiding from Humanity: Disgust, Shame, and the Law*. Princeton, NJ: Princeton University Press.

Overvold, Mark. 1984. "Morality, Self-Interest, and Reasons for Being Moral." *Philosophy and Phenomenological Research* 44: 493–507.

Parfit, Derek. 1984. *Reasons and Persons*. Oxford: Oxford University Press.

2011. *On What Matters*. Vol. 1. Oxford: Oxford University Press.

Pearce, D. W. 1983. *Cost Benefit Analysis*. 2nd. ed. London: Macmillan.

Peter, Fabienne and Hans Bernhard Schmid, eds. 2007. *Rationality and Commitment*. Oxford: Oxford University Press.

Peters, Ellen. 2006. "The Functions of Affect in the Construction of Preferences." In Slovic and Lichtenstein, eds., pp. 454–63.

Peters, Ellen, Daniel Västfjäll, Tommy Gärling, and Paul Slovic. 2006. "Affect and Decision Making: A 'Hot' Topic." *Journal of Behavioral Decision Making* 19: 79–85.

Pettit, Philip. 2002. "Decision Theory and Folk Psychology." In Philip Pettit, *Rules, Reasons and Norms*. Oxford: Oxford University Press, pp. 192–221.

Pietroski, Paul. 2000. *Causing Actions*. Oxford: Oxford University Press.

Quinn, Warren. 1995. "Putting Rationality in Its Place." In Rosalind Hursthouse, Gavin Lawrence, and Warren Quinn, eds., *Virtues and Reasons: Philippa Foot and Moral Theory*. Oxford: Clarendon Press, pp. 189–90.

Rabin, Matthew. 1993. "Incorporating Fairness into Game Theory and Economics." *American Economic Review* 83: 1281–302.

Radcliffe, David, ed., "John Ogilby." In *Lives of Scottish Poets* (1822), Part V. http://scotspoets.cath.vt.edu/select.php?select=Ogilby._John

Railton, Peter. 1986. "Facts and Values." *Philosophical Topics* 24: 5–31.

Ratneshwar, S. and David Mick, eds. 2005. *Inside Consumption: Consumer Motives, Goals, and Desires*. New York: Routledge.

Ratneshwar, S., David Mick, S. Ratneshwar, and Cynthia Huffman, eds. 2000. *Why of Consumption: Contemporary Perspectives on Consumer Motives, Goals, and Desires*. New York: Routledge.

Raz, Joseph. 1984. *The Morality of Freedom*. Oxford: Oxford University Press.

Reynolds, James and David Paris. 1979. "The Concept of 'Choice, and Arrow's Theorem." *Ethics* 89: 354–71.

Richter, Marcel. 1966. "Revealed Preference Theory." *Econometrica* 34: 635–45.

Rosen, Sherwin. 1974. "Hedonic Prices and Implicit Markets: Product Differentiation in Pure Competition." *The Journal of Political Economy* 82: 34–55.

Rubinstein, Ariel and Yuval Salant. 2008. "Some Thoughts on the Principle of Revealed Preference." In Caplin and Schotter, eds., pp. 116–24.

Sagoff, Mark. 2004. *Price, Principle, and the Environment*. Cambridge: Cambridge University Press.

Samuelson, P. 1938. "A Note on the Pure Theory of Consumers' Behaviour." *Economica* 5: 61–71.

1947. *The Foundations of Economic Analysis*. Cambridge, MA: Harvard University Press.

1950. "Evaluation of National Income." *Oxford Economic Papers* (N.S.) 2: 1–29.

Sartre, Jean-Paul. 1962. *Sketch for a Theory of the Emotions*. London: Methuen.

Savage, Leonard. 1972. *The Foundations of Statistics*. 2nd ed. New York: Dover.

Scanlon, T. M. 1998. *What We Owe to Each Other*. Cambridge, MA: Harvard University Press.

Scarantino, Andrea. 2010. "Insights and Blindspots of the Cognitive Theory of the Emotions." *British Journal for the Philosophy of Science* 61: 729–68.

Schapiro, Tamar. 2009. "The Nature of Inclination." *Ethics* 119: 229–56.

Schelling, Thomas. 2006. *Micromotives and Macrobehavior*. New York: W. W. Norton & Co.

Schneider, S. and J. Shanteau, eds. 2003. *Emerging Perspectives on Judgment and Decision Research*. Cambridge: Cambridge University Press.

Schroeder, Mark. 2007. *Slaves of the Passions*. Oxford: Oxford University Press

Scitovsky, Tibor. 1941. "A Note on Welfare Propositions in Economics." *Review of Economic Studies* 9: 77–88.

Sen, Amartya. 1970. *Collective Choice and Social Welfare*. San Francisco: Holden-Day.

1971. "Choice Functions and Revealed Preference." *Review of Economic Studies* 38: 307–17.

1973. "Behaviour and the Concept of Preference." *Economica* 40: 241–59; Rpt. and cited from Sen (1982), pp. 54–73.

1977. "Rational Fools: A Critique of the Behavioural Foundations of Economic Theory." *Philosophy & Public Affairs* 6: 317–44.

1980. "Description as Choice." *Oxford Economic Papers* 32: 353–69; Rpt. and cited from Sen (1982), pp. 432–49.

1982. *Choice, Welfare, and Measurement*. Oxford: Blackwell.

1985a. "Goals, Commitment, and Identity." Rpt. and cited from Sen (2002), pp. 206–24.

1985b. "Rationality and Uncertainty." *Theory and Decision* 18: 109–27.

1987a. *On Ethics and Economics*. Oxford: Blackwell.

1987b. *The Standard of Living*. Cambridge: Cambridge University Press.

1991a. "Opportunities and Freedoms" (from the Arrow Lectures). In Sen (2002), pp. 583–622.

1991b. "Utility: Ideas and Terminology." *Economics and Philosophy* 7: 277–84.

1993. "Internal Consistency of Choice." *Econometrica* 61: 495–521.

1997a. "Individual Preference as the Basis of Social Choice." Rpt. and cited from Sen (2002), pp. 300–24.

1997b. "Maximization and the Act of Choice." *Econometrica* 65: 745–79.

2002. *Rationality and Freedom*. Cambridge, MA: Harvard University Press.

2007. "Rational Choice: Discipline, Brand Name, and Substance." In Fabienne Peter and Hans Bernhard Schmid, eds., pp. 339–61.

Simon, Dan, Daniel C. Krawczyk, Keith J. Holyoak. 2004. "Construction of Preferences by Constraint Satisfaction." *Psychological Science* 15: 331–36.

Simon, Herbert. 1982. *Models of Bounded Rationality*. Cambridge, MA: MIT Press.

Skyrms, Brian. 1982. "Causal Decision Theory." *The Journal of Philosophy* 79: 695–711.

Slovic, Paul and Sarah Lichtenstein. 1968. "Relative Importance of Probabilities and Payoffs in Risk Taking." *Journal of Experimental Psychology Monograph* 78 (part 2): 1–18.

Sobel, D. 1998. "Well-Being as the Object of Moral Consideration." *Economics and Philosophy* 14: 249–81.

Solomon, Michael. 2004. *Consumer Behavior: Buying, Having, and Being*. 6th ed. Upper Saddle River, NJ: Pearson Prentice Hall.

Solomon, Robert. 2003. *Not Passion's Slave*. Oxford: Oxford University Press.

Stampe, Dennis. 1987. "The Authority of Desire." *Philosophical Review* 96: 335–81.

Stich, Stephen. 1983. *From Folk Psychology to Cognitive Science: The Case Against Belief*. Cambridge, MA: MIT Press.

Stigler, George and Gary Becker. 1977. "De Gustibus Non Est Disputandum." *American Economic Review* 67: 76–90.

Sugden, Robert and Alan Williams. 1978. *The Principles of Practical Cost-Benefit Analysis*. Oxford: Oxford University Press.

Sumner, L. W. 1996. *Welfare, Happiness, and Ethics*. Oxford: Clarendon Press.

Temkin, Larry. 1987. "Intransitivity and the Mere Addition Paradox." *Philosophy & Public Affairs* 16: 138–87.

Thagard, Paul. 2000. *Coherence in Thought and Action*. Cambridge, MA: MIT Press.

2006. *Hot Thought: Mechanisms and Applications of Emotional Cognition*. Cambridge, MA: MIT Press.

Thaler, Richard and Cass Sunstein. 2003a. "Libertarian Paternalism." *American Economic Review* 93:175–79.

2003b. "Libertarian Paternalism Is Not an Oxymoron." *University of Chicago Law Review* 70: 1159–202.

2008. *Nudge: Improving Decisions about Health, Wealth, and Happiness*. New Haven, CT: Yale University Press.

Tuomela, Raimo. 1977. *Human Action and Its Explanation: A Study on the Philosophical Foundations of Psychology*. Dordrecht: Reidel.

Tversky, Amos. 1969. "Intransitivity of Preferences." *Psychological Review* 84: 31–48.

Tversky, Amos and Kahneman, Daniel. 1981. "The Framing of Decisions and the Psychology of Choice." *Science* 211: 453–58.

Tversky, Amos and Richard Thaler. 1990. "Preference Reversals." *Journal of Economic Perspectives* 4: 201–11.

Varian, Hal. 1984. *Microeconomic Analysis*. New York: W. W. Norton.

2006a. *Intermediate Microeconomics: A Modern Approach*. 7th ed. New York: W.W. Norton & Company.

2006b. "Revealed Preference." In Michael Szenberg, Lall Ramrattan, and Aron Gottesman, eds., *Samuelsonian Economics and the Twenty-First Century*. Oxford: Oxford University Press, pp. 99–115.

Vining, Aidan and Weimer, David L. (2010) "An Assessment of Important Issues Concerning the Application of Benefit-Cost Analysis to Social Policy," *Journal of Benefit-Cost Analysis* 1(1): Article 6. Available at: http://www.bepress.com/jbca/vol1/iss1/6 DOI: 10.2202/2152-2812.1013.

Wakker, Peter. 2010. *Prospect Theory: For Risk and Ambiguity*. Cambridge: Cambridge University Press.

Weibull, Jörgen. 2004. "Testing Game Theory." In Steffen Huck, ed., *Advances in Understanding Strategic Behaviour, Game Theory, Experiments, and Bounded Rationality: Essays in Honor of Werner Güth*. London: Macmillan, pp. 85–104.

Wellman, Henry. 1990. *The Child's Theory of Mind*. Cambridge, MA: MIT Press.

Zerbe, Richard, Yoram Bauman, and Aaron Finkle. 2006. "An Aggregate Measure for Benefit-Cost Analysis." *Ecological Economics* 58: 449–61.

Index

Printed in the United States
By Bookmasters